THGUID

CW00351779

THE REALLY PRACTICAL GUIDE
TO
PRIMARY RE

2nd Edition

Hubert Smith

Stanley Thornes (Publishers) Ltd

Text © Hubert Smith 1990, 1996

Original line illustrations © Stanley Thornes (Publishers) Ltd 1990, 1996

All rights reserved. No part of this publication may be reproduced or transmitted in any form or by any means, electronic or mechanical, including photocopying, recording, or any information storage and retrieval system, without permission in writing from the publisher or under licence from the Copyright Licensing Agency Limited. Further details of such licences (for reprographic reproduction) may be obtained from the Copyright Licensing Agency Limited, of 90 Tottenham Court Road, London W1P 0LP.

First published in 1990 by:
Stanley Thornes (Publishers) Ltd
Ellenborough House
Wellington Street
CHELTENHAM GL50 1YW
England

Second edition published 1996

00 01 02 03 04 / 10 9 8 7 6 5 4 3 2

A catalogue record for this book is available from the British Library

ISBN 0 7487 2507 5

Typeset by Tech-Set Ltd, Gateshead, Tyne & Wear
Printed and bound in Great Britain by Redwood Books, Trowbridge, Wiltshire

Contents

Preface

The purpose of this book is not to push back the frontiers of religious education (RE), nor to say anything particularly original about it. Rather, it has two main aims:

1 To give help to class teachers who might be experiencing difficulty in handling this highly controversial and much misunderstood area of the Primary school curriculum.

2 To provide students on initial teacher-training courses with a clearer idea of what is involved in contemporary RE work. Many will have only a vague remembrance of their own childhood experience of RE in school, and many more will probably be strongly influenced by the older and now out-moded approaches of earlier years.

A great deal has happened to RE during the past quarter of a century – not only in the development of new approaches, but also in the way that its aims and intentions are to be perceived. The changes brought about by the Education Reform Act of 1988 have still not been thoroughly implemented, nor have all of the implications of that Act been thoroughly understood. There are numerous books which recount these revolutionary developments, but not very many which offer practical help in teaching this area of the curriculum. It is hoped that this book will go some way towards remedying that situation.

This new and revised edition now includes a short chapter on the Act of Collective Worship, which should clarify the distinction between the 'Assembly' and the RE work which goes on within the classroom, and help both students and practising teachers to deal more effectively with these two areas of activity. Some simple diagrams have also been added to the chapter on 'Visiting a place of worship', and the list of resources (Chapter 18) has been extended and up-dated.

Acknowledgements

My debt to others will be more than evident in the pages of this book: I have drawn upon the ideas of so many people that it is impossible to remember all of them. If I have inadvertently borrowed anything and failed to identify its source, then I apologise, and will gladly make amends if the matter is brought to my notice.

I owe special thanks to generations of students in the world of teacher training – briefly at what was then Maria Grey College in Twickenham, and far more at what is now the Anglia Polytechnic University in Brentwood, Essex.

I am grateful to the staff and children at Glebe County Junior School and Grove County Junior School, both in Rayleigh. A considerable part of what is written here was tried out there, in one way and another, and in more than a few instances was modified in the light of that experience.

Most of all I am grateful to my wife, for enduring so many hours while I sat slaving over a hot word-processor, always promising her that the project was 'nearly there'. I hope that what I have produced will make all that worthwhile, and that those who read it will find it helpful.

Hubert Smith

How to use this book

Section A sets out the basic principles underlying religious education (RE) in state schools, and explains the present legal position. Guidance is given concerning the purpose of RE within the curriculum, the place of other religions alongside Christianity, the broadened scope and content of RE today, and the ways in which RE relates to other subject areas.

Section B deals with the planning process, focusing upon the topic approach, and provides examples of possible RE programmes.

Section C gives practical advice in working out actual classroom activities, and offers suggestions concerning visiting a place of worship in the context of RE. The issue of measuring success (evaluation and assessment) is also considered.

Section D provides basic information about the major faiths of the world, and about aspects of Christianity in particular. Some useful addresses are listed, and resources are identified.

Section E examines some of the issues involved in planning and leading Acts of Collective Worship, which are technically distinct from classroom RE.

It is hoped that those who use this book will strongly resist the temptation to jump the first sections and look only at the lesson outlines: good practice becomes possible only when the principles are understood. Without that understanding, teachers will not be able to devise their own plans, nor will they really grasp the point of much that is suggested here.

It is assumed throughout that teachers will exercise freedom and professional judgement when applying what is set out in these pages. Teachers are individuals, each with his or her own strengths and weaknesses. Similarly, no two schools are exactly alike, nor are the classes and the children within them. It is impossible to legislate for the 'average' situation, because it does not exist!

BASIC PRINCIPLES

This section sets out the basic principles behind all RE in state schools, and puts the planning process into its full context. It explains:

▶ misunderstandings and misconceptions

▶ the legal position of RE today

▶ current aims and objectives

▶ the position of Christianity among the other world religions

▶ the breadth of content in contemporary RE

▶ the links between RE and the total curriculum.

WHY IS RELIGIOUS EDUCATION SUCH A PROBLEM?

Before we can begin to suggest solutions to the problems which RE presents to the busy primary teacher, it may be useful to summarise what those problems actually are. Not everyone experiences them in the same way, of course, but a survey of teachers' observations produced the following comments:

> ❝ *Religion should be taught in church or in the home, not in school. What people believe is their own private business.* ❞

> ❝ *It is impossible to teach RE without being religiously committed, and I don't go to church myself. I feel like a hypocrite, teaching children things which I don't personally believe.* ❞

> ❝ *I don't know enough about religion to be able to teach it properly – especially when I'm supposed to include other major world religions. My teacher training was very sketchy in this respect.* ❞

> ❝ *I can't see that RE has any direct relevance to the children's everyday life, except in very special circumstances. There just isn't time for it when we know that it isn't part of the National Curriculum, and there are so many other pressures to cope with.* ❞

> ❝ *I thought that the law had been relaxed, and that we were free to choose whether we teach RE or not. I must confess that I haven't taught it for ages, and no-one has said anything to me.* ❞

> ❝ *Research has proved that young children can't make any sense of religious ideas until they reach adolescence, so there's nothing that we can realistically do in the primary school.* ❞

> ❝ *We embody all our RE in the Act of Collective Worship, and of course we include moral teaching whenever the opportunity arises in normal classroom work. We think that covers it.* ❞

Every one of these statements reveals misconception and misunderstanding, and all of them can be countered in a positive way. The fact that these views are so widespread is probably a direct consequence of the speed at which things have been changing in recent years.

Obviously it is impossible here to make a thoroughgoing analysis of the nature of these changes, but we can note that developments in three main areas have affected RE in particular: these are in British society at large, in educational thinking, and in religious scholarship.

Changes in society

Since the Second World War, Britain has become a very different kind of country from what it used to be. People are much more mobile, and their ability to travel easily has resulted in the collapse of the kind of society in which all the members of the extended family lived in close proximity to one another. The local Christian church is no longer the centre of the community, and consequently its authority in that way has diminished. Only a very small proportion of the population attends a place of worship on anything like a regular basis. Teachers are therefore unable to make the kind of assumptions about the children's background that were possible in earlier times.

In addition, Britain is now a much more multi-cultural and multi-faith nation. It has often been observed that there are more Muslims in England than there are Methodists. Whereas the ethnic minorities were formerly all immigrants, today an increasingly high proportion of them have been born in this country, and their religious customs have thus become a part of our native culture. They have the right to be taken fully into account in the content and the presentation of RE.

At a somewhat different level, it is fair to say that people today are generally better educated and more self-confident than was the case a few generations ago. They are less ready to accept authority without question. Although the rejection of authority can bring with it many problems, at the same time there is in our contemporary society an openness and an honesty which make dogmatic teaching of the old style virtually impossible. The teacher in the modern classroom is much more likely to be questioned, and cannot adopt the authoritarian style which was so characteristic of education during the first half of the present century.

Changes in educational thinking

Much more is known today about the ways in which children think and learn. Few would still wish to picture children as empty vessels, waiting to be filled up with knowledge dispensed by a wise teacher addressing them from the front of the class, while they themselves sit dutifully in rows. The emphasis now is upon exploration and experience, instead of upon instruction. The child, rather than the subject matter, is placed firmly in the centre of the learning process. We shall see in a later chapter how this has affected RE in particular.

Changes in religious scholarship

A great deal has happened during this century in the field of religious scholarship, as a result of the rise of the 'critical' approach. The word 'critical' does not imply that scholars are now doubting everything: it means that they try to look objectively at their subject-matter, using the knowledge and evidence at their disposal. In other words, they look at it 'scientifically'. Perhaps the most conspicuous development from this has been the general recognition that the Bible is actually a collection of ancient religious documents, written by human beings, and edited and preserved over many centuries. It is still reverenced as sacred scripture among Christians, but there is now open acknowledgement that it was never meant to be a children's story book, and that it cannot be employed in the unquestioningly literal fashion that was formerly prevalent. The idea that if something is 'in the Bible' it must therefore be true in every sense has largely faded away, and with it has gone that style of teaching in which the Bible was employed as the final and infallible arbiter of truth.

Changes like these are not merely passing trends, likely to be reversed at any moment. Rather, they reflect the ways in which things in general have been (and still are) moving, and in the field of education they have to be recognised and accepted. RE, like all the other areas of the school curriculum, has to be taught within this atmosphere of change. It is unrealistic to present it as a bulwark of permanence in an otherwise unstable world, or to teach it as if it has been left untouched by the passing of time. It is hoped that in the following chapters some light will be shed upon how teachers can be enabled to cope with this new, exciting, and to some extent daunting situation.

CHAPTER
2

WHAT THE LAW REQUIRES

No discussion of RE in state schools can really be appreciated until the legal position is fully understood. There are certain things which are required to be done, and there are other things which are actually illegal. The law strongly influences what can happen in classroom RE. The Education Reform Act (1988) has introduced some important changes in the law, and these need to be outlined and explained. It was the 1944 Education Act (the 'Butler' Act) which laid the foundations upon which this legislation has been based, and much of it has been left untouched, but certain parts have been modified or clarified. There are also some matters which are quite new. The following summary outlines the general position as it is today.

RE must be taught in all state-maintained schools

The compulsory nature of RE, as set out in the 1944 Education Act, remains unchanged. It must be provided for all pupils who are in attendance at the school, and in the last resort legal action may be taken against any Local Education Authority (LEA) which fails to ensure that this obligation is fulfilled in the schools which are under its jurisdiction. The Local Education Authority itself is empowered to discipline any headteacher who neglects to see to it that RE is taught in every class, because that is part of his or her contractual duties.

RE must be in accordance with an Agreed Syllabus

The law stipulates that RE must be taught in accordance with principles and policies determined by the LEA, and set out in the form of an Agreed Syllabus. It is called 'agreed' because before it can be approved for use in schools it has to receive the agreement of a specially convened committee, known as the Standing Advisory Council on Religious Education. This Council, widely referred to by its initials SACRE, has a range of important responsibilities. In order to reflect as many as possible of the viewpoints regarding RE, it is made up of representatives from four groups:

(1) The Church of England, as the established church of this country
(2) Such other Christian and other religious denominations as will appropriately reflect the principal traditions in the area
(3) Teachers' professional associations
(4) The Local Authority itself.

Because every LEA is responsible for providing its own Agreed Syllabus, inevitably there are likely to be differences between these publications across the country as a whole, except in those cases where one Authority has adopted the Agreed Syllabus of another. However, most have the same general philosophy in terms of how they see the aims and objectives of RE, because they usually reflect current thinking in the country at large, rather than localised opinion. Some of the latest syllabuses have departed from tradition by giving schools greater freedom to devise their own RE programmes while remaining within the boundaries set down in the formal statement of principles.

RE is part of the 'basic' but not the 'National' Curriculum

Every school has to ensure that the basic curriculum is provided for all pupils, but within that there is a subdivision known as the National Curriculum, for which nationally prescribed attainment targets have been set. These targets do not apply to RE, because it is not part of the National Curriculum as such. However, it is open to Local Education Authorities to set their own attainment targets for RE if they so wish, and naturally these are likely to match the requirements laid down in the local Agreed Syllabuses. Teachers may therefore find that they are expected to meet two distinct sets of targets – one for the National Curriculum subjects, and another one (devised locally but with the same legal force) emerging from their LEA. In short, although RE is not actually listed among the areas within the National Curriculum, it does in effect have much the same kind of status.

The 'conscience clauses'

As was the case under the terms of the 1944 Education Act, all parents have the right to withdraw their children from RE lessons if they wish to do so, and all teachers (including headteachers) have the right to refuse to teach RE. It is the only area of the entire school curriculum in which this right applies.

It is a pity that the term 'conscience clauses' ever came into vogue, because as a matter of fact conscience does not really enter into it at all. Neither parents nor teachers are actually required to give any reason for their request to withdraw, and there need be no conscientious element in their decision. The only thing that is necessary is for the arrangement to be formalised, and where such an application is properly made to a headteacher, it cannot be refused. Nor can any teacher or parent be penalised for making it. The headteacher cannot reject the application on the ground that he or she thinks it is unjustified, although there is no reason why the matter should not be discussed in a professional manner.

Parents who wish their children to follow a different form of religious teaching from that offered within the school cannot insist that an alternative be provided. The school has fulfilled its legal obligations by offering what is set out in the Agreed Syllabus. If the parents want something else, they have to provide it themselves at their own expense, though the LEA must allow it to take place on school premises, provided that it is not an unreasonable request, and that the alternative is unavailable locally.

It has to be admitted that where such withdrawals are made there can be some awkward practical problems raised. If a child is opted out by his or her parents from the RE lesson, then difficulties are encountered when the school day is not divided up into traditional subject compartments. It is now general practice in primary schools, with a few exceptions, to organise the learning in an integrated way through the 'topic' method. Thus it is not easy to withdraw a child because the RE may be inextricably bound up with another area of the curriculum. Similarly, a teacher who wishes not to teach RE will need to be replaced by someone else, and this is not always a simple matter to arrange. If, in an extreme case, all the teachers in a particular school decided to opt out of RE, then it would be open to the headteacher to find an unqualified replacement to carry out the obligatory work. The Government Department for Education has made it plain that LEAs and schools must always keep in mind their duty to comply with requests for withdrawal when they are determining the ways in which both RE and the Act of Collective Worship are being organised.

Occasionally children will raise spontaneous and unexpected religious questions at times when other areas of the curriculum are being taught. The 'official' view of this is that parents would not be able to insist upon withdrawing their child every time such a question is raised, since the teacher's response does not constitute RE within the meaning of the law.

The content of RE must reflect Britain's Christian tradition

The recent legislation has made it plain that all Agreed Syllabuses – and therefore by implication all RE teaching in state schools – shall reflect the fact that the religious traditions in Great Britain are in the main Christian. The effect of this is to remind teachers that they must place their emphasis upon the presentation of the Christian religion, showing children the ways in which it has influenced British history and culture. The wording of the Act here, however, is somewhat loose, and it still remains to be seen how it will generally be interpreted. But it is also stressed that proper account should be taken of the beliefs and practices of the other principal religions represented in this country. As we have seen, these other faiths have a voice in the Standing Advisory Councils, and can influence the nature and the contents of the Agreed Syllabus.

There are schools in Britain in which the majority of pupils are drawn from non-Christian backgrounds, and this is particularly true of London and other large cities where there is a high concentration of people from ethnic minorities. The needs of such schools are met by allowing, in the law, for a substantial element of teaching about other religions, but the rule about teaching the tradition of Christianity still remains.

RE must be taught in an unbiased way

Any syllabus, agreed or otherwise, cannot take away from the teacher that special professional freedom of judgement needed to determine how anything shall be taught. But the Education Reform Act, like its earlier counterpart, insists that teachers may not present RE in a way which is distinctive of any particular religious denomination. This is another way of saying that the 'party line' of any religious group may not be presented to children as if it were the main or the only viewpoint. But this does not mean that the characteristics of particular churches or religions cannot be mentioned; indeed, it is important that they should be taught, but it must be done objectively, such as when making comparisons between one kind of church and another. What is *not* permitted is for the teacher to adopt the catechism or doctrinal standpoint of a specific denomination and neglect to show that there are others equally deserving of respect.

Church schools have separate legislation

There are many schools throughout Britain which were set up by voluntary bodies, and the great majority of these are church schools, linked with particular denominations. They fall into two main groups. There are 'voluntary aided' schools, and there are 'voluntary controlled' schools. The distinction between them has to do with the degree of support provided by the state. An aided school is one in which the religious foundation has the greater stake. A controlled school is one in which the state has the main responsibility, and in practice it is hardly distinguishable from a county school. For the purposes of RE, however, there is an important distinction in law. In an aided school, the RE is taught in accordance with a syllabus laid down by the religious body, but in a controlled school the LEA Agreed Syllabus must be followed – unless the parents specifically request that their children are taught in accordance with the other one. In other words, a controlled school is likely to have two separate RE syllabuses, one which reflects the ideas of the church, and the other which is produced by the Local Education Authority. In theory (though it appears that it hardly ever happens in practice) a teacher could be in the odd position of having to teach in accordance with two different sets of guidelines, which may or may not be in harmony with each other.

RE in an integrated curriculum

Where a school operates on the basis of an 'integrated day', in which several subject-areas are merged together – possibly within a chosen topic – it is important that the RE element remains identifiable. It must also be sufficiently substantial to meet the legal requirements. For example, the law does not recognise, as genuine RE, an occasional fleeting religious reference which does no more than pay lip-service to the demands of the Agreed Syllabus. As with any other subject-area in the normal curriculum, it must be possible to identify the RE component, justify its inclusion, match it to the requirements of the Agreed Syllabus and assess the extent to which the pupils have learned from it, e.g., by reference to any locally determined attainment targets.

The whole issue of adequate coverage of RE is of particular importance in relation to the Act of Collective Worship and such other activities as Nativity Plays, carol concerts, or art work related to religious festivals. As we shall see in Section E of this book, it is technically illegal to reduce the amount of RE work done in the classroom on the ground that it is being sufficiently catered for in the 'Assembly'. Equally, it is not permissible to argue that such activities as the making of Christmas decorations for the classroom or the rehearsal of new carols can count as RE, unless these activities are accompanied by such things as a genuine exploration of celebratory customs or the place of music in religious worship.

The main purpose of the law relating to RE is that it shall give support to an area of the curriculum which the state has judged to be important. The point is that RE is to be taught, not simply because the law says so, but because a child's education is incomplete without some appreciation of the religious dimension of life.

CHAPTER 3

WHAT IS THE PURPOSE OF RELIGIOUS EDUCATION?

We have noted that RE has changed a great deal since the 1944 Education Act, and have highlighted the three main reasons for this – changes in society, in educational thinking, and in the field of religious scholarship. But without any doubt the most important change of all has been in the way that the aims and objectives of RE have come to be perceived. It now has an entirely different purpose: whereas it formerly sought to bring children into membership of the Christian church, today it is justified as part of the curriculum solely on educational grounds, and this is reflected in the fact that in the new Education Reform Act it is called religious education and not religious instruction. We can actually trace the line of development in the changing aims of RE by noting how its title has evolved through the past few generations.

Religious instruction

The word 'instruction' carried with it overtones of authoritarianism. It epitomised what was then the general intention behind the teaching of religion – or, more accurately, of Christianity in particular, and that was to initiate pupils into the life of the Christian fellowship. It was essentially a form of evangelism, carried out upon a captive audience. We can see this very clearly in a quotation from the 1944 version of the Sunderland Agreed Syllabus, which is typical of the great majority published around that time:

> **❝** *The teacher will strive to bring the pupils into such vital contact with the religious experience of mankind as recorded in the Bible and elsewhere that there will be aroused in them a desire to worship the God whose dealings with men they have been learning, and to present those experiences in such a way that there will be born a desire to be actively and permanently associated with the Christian community.* **❞**
>
> County Borough of Sunderland Agreed Syllabus (1944)

It was this kind of approach and intention which gave rise to protests about 'indoctrination'. Although the language of such protests was somewhat highly coloured and emotive, there was more than an element of truth in it.

10

Scripture

Another popular name for RE, and one which still lives on, was 'Scripture'. This gave the game away entirely. It exposed the fact that the content of RE was predominantly the Christian Bible. Early Agreed Syllabuses were almost exclusively concerned with mapping out a programme of Bible study, based on the assumption that the scriptures would somehow speak for themselves and gradually draw the children into Christian discipleship. Little scope was offered for pupils to make a genuine *analysis* of the Biblical material, and the most common approach was to employ it in the service of moral teaching, aimed at showing children the difference between right and wrong. Even today some teachers find it hard to break free of the habit of looking for a Bible story which they can attach to a theme or topic in order to turn it into RE.

The need for change

With the passing of time it became clear that Bible-based RE was not producing the hoped-for results. Pupils were leaving school, not with a sound foundation of understanding but with a very patchy and incoherent awareness of what the Bible contained or meant. The work of Ronald Goldman in the 1960s brought things to a head:

> ❝ *Various surveys have indicated that at the end of secondary schooling knowledge of the Bible and even of what Christians believe is appallingly poor. Ignorance of many of the Christian festivals, the parables of Jesus and the nature of the prophets, and an incredible vagueness about the chronological order of well-known events in the New and Old Testaments, all indicate that despite the Bible teaching received after ten years or more under the Agreed Syllabuses, little of it seems to have registered . . . the Bible is not a children's book . . . the teaching of it may do more damage than good to a child's religious understanding . . . too much biblical material is used too soon and too frequently.* ❞

Goldman, R., *Readiness for Religion* (Routledge and Kegan Paul, 1964)

Goldman was not criticising the aims and objectives of RE at that time, but the methods, and in particular those which did not take account of the children's real-life situation. He judged that it was starting in the wrong place, and he tried to rectify this by proposing an approach which started where the child actually is, and not where it was considered that he or she ought to be. This was fully in line with the growing feeling at that time among educationists that all true learning must be child-centred rather than subject-based.

The child-centred approach

The aims of RE shifted when it was realised that the child-centred approach had serious implications for an understanding of the actual *purpose* as well as for the methods of teaching this area of the curriculum. Respecting the children meant recognising that, in state schools in particular, they had to be free to grow up into a world which has within it a rich variety of religious beliefs and customs; they could not be treated as raw material for recruitment into church membership. Their need was to grow – to be educated rather than trained. 'Exploration' became one of the key words in schools, implying that learning was a matter of reaching out into unfamiliar territory, as well as being initiated into what was already familiar and traditional.

The situation today

It is now accepted that if RE is to have a proper place and status within the secular school curriculum it must be justified on educational rather than on religious grounds. There is a much clearer awareness today of the important distinction between the respective roles of the state school and the religious communities – what used to be referred to as the partnership between the day school and the Sunday school. There is also an increasing recognition that it is no part of the secular school's responsibility to indulge in religious missionary work. Gone, too, is the assumption that a teacher must necessarily be a committed religious believer in order to handle RE. What matters most is that he or she shall be professionally competent, and equipped with sufficient knowledge and skills to teach in an objective and balanced way.

Against this background, then, we can now summarise the contemporary aims of RE, and these are set out in the box below. They will be referred to frequently throughout the rest of this book.

The contemporary aims of RE

1 To provide children with an insight into the nature of religion, and what it means to be religious.
2 To help children to acquire and develop those skills which will enable them to appreciate religious ideas and practices.
3 To make available factual information about religion and religious phenomena.
4 To encourage attitudes of openness and sensitivity towards people whose religious beliefs and customs may be different from their own.
5 To provide in particular an awareness of the nature and claims of the Christian religion, and of the part which it has played in shaping the cultural and social life of Britain.
6 To help children to identify those areas of human life and experience in which religion plays a significant part.
7 To explore with children the relation between religion and other areas of experience and knowledge.
8 To foster a sense of awe, respect and wonder, leading to a desire to penetrate more deeply into those areas with which religion is concerned.
9 With other areas of the curriculum, to contribute towards the children's moral development.

The above aims are, of course, the overall targets of RE throughout both the primary and the secondary stages of schooling. The particular role of the primary teacher is to lay the foundations upon which further building can take place. Virtually all Agreed Syllabuses now provide, as their point of departure, a statement of how the aims of RE are understood and interpreted. Broadly speaking they will match those identified above, though inevitably there will be differences of emphasis and expression. In our later discussion of programme planning in RE (see Section B) we shall return to these aims in a more direct way.

CHAPTER 4

CHRISTIANITY AND OTHER RELIGIONS

The Education Reform Act of 1988 stipulates that in all maintained schools RE teaching shall 'reflect the fact that the religious traditions in Great Britain are in the main Christian'. But it then goes on to add that account should also be taken of 'the teaching and practices of the other principal religions represented in Great Britain'. In other words, while the teaching of RE must make plain the fact that Christianity is the traditional faith of this country, other religions should nevertheless have a place in the RE programme. So we therefore have to consider what this implies and how such an approach might be implemented.

There have been 'other religions' in Britain for a long time, and some of them have become very well established. Jewish people have been here for centuries, and in larger cities places of worship were being built long ago to meet the needs of migrant workers and visitors from a variety of lands. More recently, successive waves of immigration have brought people from such places as the Indian sub-continent and the Afro-Caribbean world, as well as from China and Hong Kong. All this has resulted not only in the establishment of different religious and cultural practices, but also in the growth of distinctive styles within Christianity itself, well illustrated by the lively services of worship associated with the West Indian communities.

The pattern of settlement has been irregular. The great majority of people who follow non-Christian religions are to be found in or near the main cities and sea-ports, while in small towns and rural areas they are much fewer in number. Slowly the picture is changing, but the situation is still such that, by living in one part of the country as distinct from another, one can easily gain a false view of what is happening in Britain as a whole. A resident in Southall sees a very different social scene from that observed by someone living in a Shropshire village.

We noted earlier that changes in British society have had a marked effect upon education in general and upon RE in particular. The social and religious make-up of the various parts of the country has profoundly affected the way RE is taught. In those areas which are multi-ethnic, the non-Christian faiths are generally included as a natural part of the curriculum because they are a real feature of the life of the school and its immediate environment. But in areas which are usually classified as 'all-white' it is quite a different story. There is often a reluctance to include much reference to other religious cultures simply because, as one teacher put it, 'we don't have that problem here'.

This latter view must be seriously questioned. The presence of minority cultures within a school classroom is not a problem at all, but a golden opportunity for the teacher to extend the children's horizons. A school in which all the children come from similar backgrounds is always at risk of becoming insular and parochial in its outlook, so that to teach about the wider world becomes all the more important and urgent. To enable the children to explore other people's religions is to let them adventure out into the world at large and see what life looks like from a completely different perspective. Some of them will encounter this outside world through the medium of television or family holidays abroad, but there will be much that remains mysterious to them if they have no real awareness of the differences of religious outlook that distinguish one culture from another.

Recognising past mistakes

It has to be admitted that there are serious issues to be faced by the teacher who wants to adopt a multi-faith approach to RE as well as to all the other areas of the curriculum. Among those issues is that of deciding upon the most appropriate ways of introducing non-Christian religions, especially to younger children. When world religions first became a significant feature of RE teaching round about 1960, teachers had no real precedents upon which to build their planning, because until that time RE had been almost exclusively Christian in approach and content. The enthusiasm for this broader concept of RE was undoubted, but very often eagerness outstripped wisdom, with some unfortunate results. In retrospect we can now see where mistakes were made, and what can be learned from them, by summarising certain of the approaches adopted.

The 'comparative religion' approach

At first the term 'comparative religion' was widely employed to describe the approach to world faiths, but it was a misleading concept, and it had the effect of sending many teachers off in what proved to be the wrong direction. It gave the impression that the main purpose was to show pupils a range of religious beliefs and life-styles, which could then be compared with one another so as to identify which was the best. Because of the Christian tradition in which RE had been presented in the past, the hope was that they would choose Christianity – and in case they were attracted to a different faith the teacher was sometimes advised to give a gentle push in the desired direction. Thus, as early as 1944, we find this in the Agreed Syllabus of the County Borough of Sunderland:

> **"** *This review of the great religions of the world should lead us to see that whatever is good in these religions . . . is found unified and elevated in the Christian religion.* **"**
>
> County Borough of Sunderland Agreed Syllabus (1944)

The approach came close to being a kind of window-shopping among the world's faith systems, with Christianity used as the standard by which they were judged. It quickly became evident, however, that this was a very biased way of teaching, and that it was unfair to the great non-Christian traditions. Today the term 'comparative religion' has dropped out of favour, though it is still encountered from time to time.

The 'peculiarities' approach

Another common mistake was that of presenting to children only the most exotic and sensational aspects of other religious traditions, which of course made them look very strange indeed – so

15

strange, in fact, that children were sometimes heard to ask why these religions ever attracted any followers at all. Islam, for instance, was frequently portrayed as a mixture of whirling dervishes and hard-line legalists who chopped off hands for what, in our own culture, seemed relatively minor offences. Again, Buddhists were pictured as saffron-robed monks, setting themselves on fire in busy Oriental streets. Such caricatures naturally aroused the indignation of the people who actually belonged to these traditions, and they were not slow in making their views known. The lesson learned from this was the importance of presenting an accurate and balanced picture which avoided distortion and caricature.

The 'evolutionary' approach

Equally misguided was the tendency in some quarters to imply that the various religions of the world fitted into a kind of evolutionary scale of development. Reference was often made to 'higher' and 'lower' religions, and the word 'primitive' was used in a way which suggested crudity and ignorance. There was an unverified assumption made that all religions were really heading in the same direction ('We all worship the same God, don't we?'), but that some had travelled further than others – and, of course, once again Christianity was the religion which had reached the final goal. But more serious study of the great faiths of mankind has shown that this outlook cannot be sustained because it does not fit the real facts.

The 'differences' approach

Here, the practice was to concentrate almost exclusively upon the differences between the various religions, usually at the expense of the things that they share in common. Obviously important differences do exist, and it certainly is a part of the teacher's task to expose them; but it was quickly discovered that when the differences alone were highlighted the result was the creation of a 'them-and-us' attitude, which did little or nothing for genuine understanding or mutual respect. Very often, too, it was not made clear that the differences were frequently not so much of religious belief as of cultural tradition.

The 'living and dead religions' approach

It is obviously true that some religions have lost their vitality and are no longer actively followed. They are interesting as history but not as much more than that. These are sometimes referred to as 'dead' religions, and one thinks for instance of the Greek myths or ancient Egyptian sun-worship. Unfortunately, some world religions were taught in a way which suggested that they too were 'dead', when in reality they are still very much alive, playing an important part in people's lives. Even Christianity itself has not escaped this kind of treatment. The teacher who takes children to visit an empty church building, and focuses all or most of their attention upon its past history, is leaving them with the feeling that no-one ever uses the place nowadays. But probably no religion has suffered more in this respect than Judaism. Because it is the parent religion of Christianity and (in a different way) also of Islam, it has often been presented to children as if it died giving birth. Teachers have constantly treated Judaism as if it had nothing more to contribute after the arrival of Jesus, thus effectively obscuring the fact that it is still a vital and living way of life for millions of people across the world. Even today one still encounters teachers who use contemporary Jewish artefacts such as prayer-shawls or Passover plates under the mistaken impression that they are providing background to the life of Jesus ('This is what Jesus would have done when he was a boy . . .').

The 'geographical' approach

In the early days of teaching about world religions it was both customary and understandable for teachers to link particular faiths with their country of origin. Islam was thus presented against the backcloth of the Arabian or the Indian world, and it appeared to children that all Sikhs live in the Punjab. But times and circumstances have changed tremendously. Many of the adherents of these faiths, and others, are British-born, and they practise their faith in this country. It is becoming increasingly irrelevant to introduce other religions through lessons about life in Pakistan or the West Indies, though this can be useful with older children, when exploring how and where these faiths came into being. Younger children, however, seeing these religions manifested within their own immediate locality, will be helped much more if they can come to understand that they are a part of life here in Britain, rather than picturing them as intrusions from overseas.

The 'intellectual' approach

It took quite a long time for teachers to appreciate that a religious tradition is best described and interpreted by those who actually belong to it, rather than by those who stand on the outside looking in. Most of the early books about world religions were written by people who had an academic knowledge of them, and who perhaps had observed them being practised, but who lacked the experience which derives from being a committed believer. So their accounts tended to be somewhat cold and dispassionate, without the fervour and sensitivity which come only when one actually belongs to a particular tradition. Judaism as evidenced by a Jew, or Hinduism as seen by a Hindu, is likely to be more authentic than the picture painted by someone who knows the religion only from a distance.

The 'wait until later' approach

Finally there was at first widespread uncertainty about the most appropriate time for introducing children to world religions. A glance at the early Agreed Syllabuses will show that, almost without exception, non-Christian faiths were left untouched until pupils had reached the upper range of the secondary school. The general view was that younger children would not be able to appreciate or understand 'foreign' beliefs. But this clearly exposed the underlying assumption about what was involved in teaching about other faiths. It was taken for granted that at the heart of any religion lies its doctrines, which would be beyond the reach of young children. But, as we will see in Chapter 5, there is much more to a religion than beliefs. There are other aspects or dimensions which certainly *can* be presented to children at a much younger age. As this has come to be recognised, so also the teaching of world religions has found its way into the primary school, even at infant level. In addition, it is acknowledged now that Christianity is itself a world religion, and that the teaching of it has to be subject to the same ground rules as would apply when teaching any other faith system. If a young child can cope with aspects of Christianity, then by the same token he or she can cope with similar features of another religious tradition.

Approaching multi-faith RE today

Many mistakes, then, were made in the past, as teachers attempted to get to grips with what was for them a new and strange field of enquiry. Building upon the lessons learned, it is now possible to see positive approaches emerging, and we can summarise them as follows:

Teach each religion in its own right

Rather than attempting to set the world's religions alongside one another for purposes of comparison, it is better to treat each one in its own right as a coherent tradition. This enables the children to appreciate that they are not being invited to select the best or the truest, nor are they indulging in a 'pick and mix' activity: they are being helped to understand and respect beliefs and customs which belong together in a coherent pattern of religious life, and which mean a great deal to a large number of people. This does not mean that comparisons should not or cannot be drawn: indeed, sometimes they are helpful ways into clearer understanding, and it is often very revealing to take a theme (such as 'Initiation Rites' or 'Festivals') and explore it in a cross-religious manner. But what the principle *does* mean is that making comparisons *for the sole purpose of value judgements* is generally invidious, and should be avoided. Religions cannot be measured in terms of the extent to which they conform or fail to conform to the norms of Christianity.

Avoid caricaturing religions

All religions, when studied solely on the basis of isolated beliefs and customs plucked out of context, can be made to look very odd. It is the easiest thing in the world to caricature a religion by picking on some special or exotic feature. As we shall see in our next chapter, a religion has several aspects or dimensions, and each has to be seen alongside the others if it is to be properly appreciated. Teachers are advised to make as full a study as possible of the chosen faith system before attempting to introduce it to the children. By doing this a more balanced view can be gained, and the seeming eccentricities can be seen for what they really are. There are now plenty of sound books available to which teachers can refer, and there are also many excellent publications written especially for children. Some of these will be found listed in the final section of this book. If need be, someone who is actually a member of the religious tradition could be asked to check that the case is being accurately and fairly presented.

Present the contemporary picture

With the departure of the 'evolutionary' approach to world religions, the ground has been cleared for presenting them as they actually are today. Some historical background is obviously necessary in order to set the scene, and certain religions do in fact regard their own history as sacred in itself, that is, it is actually a part of the religion and not just a preamble to it. They preserve it in their traditions and customs, and pass it on to each succeeding generation. But as a general rule it is recommended that teachers try to steer away from starting their presentation with a survey of history – what has been called 'taking a running jump at it' – and try instead to examine the present-day situation. Just as we do not necessarily come to understand a person by finding out about his infancy, so also we do not necessarily form a clear picture of a contemporary religion by looking at what it used to be like. It may have changed a good deal since it began: twentieth century Christianity, for example, is very different from what it was in the days of the first apostles, and the same applies to other faiths.

Emphasise similarities rather than differences

Although the world's religions are not all the same, either on the surface or beneath it, nevertheless they do have sufficient in common for us to be able to recognise that they *are* religions. They may have different foundations, and they may have been affected by the different cultural traditions within the lands where they have flourished, but they still share certain features which bind them together. They all adopt attitudes towards life and its purpose, even though those attitudes may not be the same. They all have rituals, rules, teachings and other features which sometimes echo those found in other faith systems. It is a sound principle that these likenesses, rather than the differences, should form the starting point for understanding. Fundamental human needs and characteristics are central to all religious traditions – the need for security, for food, for love, for health, and so on. The children can begin by considering some of the things that all human beings share, no matter what their background may be: they live in homes, they belong to family groups, they eat and drink, they wear clothes, they play games, they communicate with one another, they sing, and they celebrate. It is by exploring the ways in which these basic things are done that we begin to see their importance within life in general, and within religious life in particular. If the teacher starts with these basic areas of shared concern, then the differences can be introduced more meaningfully later on.

Stress contemporary religious activity

To treat any religion as if it were no longer active or significant is really a mark of disrespect. It is a way of saying, or at least of implying, that even though there are people who still go along with these ways, they are really clinging to something dead and gone. In short, they are behind the times and they are foolish. Now if, among the aims of RE, the intention is to encourage children to respect other people's beliefs and customs, then it is important that the teacher should present them as having significance today. They matter to the people who hold to them. Children need to know what it is that Christians, Muslims, Jews, Sikhs and the rest actually do today as they go about the observance of their religion. How are their lives affected? What goes on within their homes and inside their meeting places? How do they put their religion into practice? These are the questions which matter, because it is in contemporary religious activity that the vitality of a religion is seen most plainly.

Portray Britain as a multi-faith country

Because Britain now has among its citizens people from a wide variety of religious backgrounds (as well as from no religion at all), the focus of attention has to shift away from exploring those religions in terms of their country of origin, and move towards seeing them in their contemporary British setting. Although the process of integration is still in its early stages, nevertheless there is an evident lessening of the influence of India, or the Afro-Caribbean world, or the Middle East in the religious life of these 'new Britons'. Many have never set foot outside the British Isles. There are now such things as British Islam and British Hinduism, and these are becoming increasingly distinct from the forms practised in other lands. Children now need to find out about Hindu families living in London or Birmingham, and about Muslims living in Leeds, Bradford or Whitechapel. The links with the country of origin are still strong, but with each successive generation those links become more fragile, and the impact of British life upon the religion becomes more evident. In schools where there are children from ethnic minority groups it is important that their religion should not be presented in such a way as to make it appear that the children themselves are foreigners; it is quite likely that they and their parents were born here and are struggling to win recognition as full members of our society. Much can be done to support them by letting the children see that religious diversity is a normal feature of our contemporary society.

Remember to teach from first-hand experience

We have already noted that a religion looks very different when seen from the inside rather than from the outside, and that the most authentic presentation of it is likely to come from its adherents. However, a teacher who is not a Christian, or a Muslim, or a Jew can still effectively teach about these faiths, *provided that he or she draws upon legitimate sources*. Many of the major religions which have established themselves in Britain have set up their own education departments, which not only serve their own people but also disseminate the kind of information and materials which teachers need to present the faiths in an accurate and sensitive fashion. Some of these are listed in the addresses at the end of this book, and teachers are encouraged to make enquiries about what is available to help them in their teaching. If there is a local centre such as a mosque or a synagogue accessible to the school, then of course that too will become an important resource, often able to provide help.

Emphasise the practical side of world religions with young children

The notion that children could learn about Christianity at an early age, but not about any other religion, has now been discredited; and the consequence is that world religions have found their way into the infant and junior school curriculum, instead of being left aside until the secondary stage. With that change there has come the recognition that the best starting point is not with matters of doctrine and belief, but rather with more immediate and concrete issues. The best place to begin is with the things that appear on the surface of religious life – religious clothes, religious customs, religious objects, religious buildings, and even religious people. These are what the children see first of all, and these are the things which prompt them to ask questions later on. They will not at first be able to probe at any depth, and they will be mystified by talk about things 'having a meaning'. It is clear that young children do not know what 'meaning' means. But they will be fascinated by what people do, and by things that they can see or handle. These concrete things are the 'alphabet' which has to be learned before genuine RE takes place, and it is at this level that the primary teacher makes the most effective and valuable contribution.

Agnosticism and atheism

We cannot escape from the fact that in British society today there are large numbers of people for whom formal religion has little or no part to play in their personal lives. They may be agnostics, which means that they simply have no real knowledge of religion or have not made up their minds about it; or they may be atheists, which means that they have positively concluded that there is no God, and that religion is a mistaken or false view. In practice these two often merge.

Acknowledging the presence of these within our society implies two things. It implies that their views, like other views of religion, must be respected: and it further implies that their position must be included within a balanced presentation of RE. It would be both dishonest and untrue to suggest to the children that everyone is religious in one way or another, when quite manifestly that is not the case. Even worse, it would be wrong to suggest that unbelief is somehow wicked, a view which prevailed until comparatively recently but which no longer holds any force. Honest doubt is not a sin!

But how does a teacher handle the issue of unbelief? Certainly not by suggesting to the children that this is really a question of 'science versus religion', an approach which experience has shown to be quite widespread. It is far too simplistic to claim that modern scientific thinking is the root cause of unbelief. There are many eminent scientists who are deeply religious people, and there are many others who have found that their scientific discoveries have drawn them closer to a religious outlook, rather than further away from it.

The roots of unbelief seem to lie, not in scientific thinking, but in the atmosphere of open enquiry and freedom of thought which is a characteristic of the present age. People are generally more honest about what they think, and more ready to work out their ideas for themselves. In Chapter 1 we noted that this was one of the changes that could be observed in modern society, which has brought with it a rejection of authoritarianism and dogmatism. The issue of unbelief, therefore, is best handled at primary level by creating within the school the kind of atmosphere in which children feel free to explore for themselves, without the suspicion that they are being conditioned, or that they have no real choice in deciding what is true and what is not. It should be made plain from the outset that not everyone is religious, and that the religions being presented in the classroom are open to discussion and enquiry in a completely free way. Simple statements such as 'Some people believe this, but others don't' are usually sufficient to maintain this open-ended atmosphere, and to reassure the children that they are not being required to accept something which they cannot in honesty make their own.

CHAPTER 5

THE SCOPE AND CONTENT OF RE TODAY

Probably the most distinctive feature of contemporary RE, when compared with earlier approaches, is its breadth. It ranges far more widely than it did 50 years ago. As we have seen, one reason for this is the acceptance of other religions into its repertoire, alongside Christianity. But another equally significant development has come about through the recognition that there is more to a religion than its teachings – something which was highlighted in the 1960s by Ninian Smart.

The 'six dimensions' of religion

It was in his analysis of the nature of religion that Ninian Smart made his greatest impact upon RE. He agreed that religion is very difficult to define, but he argued that this should not prevent us from trying to *describe* it. He observed that in all religions there are certain identifiable features or aspects which he referred to as 'dimensions', and he listed six of these:

> Ritual
> Mythological
> Doctrinal
> Ethical
> Social
> Experiential.

It is worth looking in some detail at each of these in turn, because together they have proved to be a very useful guide when thinking about the scope and content of RE. Obviously we must not regard Smart's analysis as being the final word on the subject: others might view religion rather differently, or extend the list further. But he has provided a valuable clue to the range of possibilities open to the teacher. (For a rounded view of Ninian Smart's analysis readers can consult *The Religious Experience of Mankind* [Collins Fontana Library, 1971].)

The ritual dimension

All religions contain customs and practices which can be generally described as rituals. These include such things as initiation, marriage or funeral rites, services of worship, and so on. Some are very simple, and others are very elaborate. Even those religions which have attempted to keep ritual to a minimum (such as Sikhism) have not managed to dispense with it altogether, because it is deeply embedded in human life, and frequently appears outside religion as well as inside.

Many social customs, such as shaking hands on meeting, or applauding by clapping hands, are actually rituals.

If we think of rituals in the broader sense as regulated patterns of behaviour, rather than being just forms of words spoken in worship (which is what the word 'ritual' strictly means), then we can see that these would include the customs found in religious festivals, holy days, naming ceremonies, and a host of other special activities. Within the rituals there lie certain clues to the beliefs which prompt people to behave in these ways. A ritual which has lost its way, that is to say, one in which the reasons for doing it have been forgotten, is what we are describing when we use the word 'superstition', and even an exploration of these can be a valuable approach to RE with older children.

In contemporary RE, much attention has been paid to rituals, festivals and ceremonies, because they have proved to be a very fruitful source of teaching material. They make up much of the outward manifestation of religion, and therefore they have a particular appeal to younger children, who, as we have noted, tend to start with the things that are on the surface before they can penetrate more deeply. It is important, however, that at some stage the children are given an opportunity to probe into why these things are done, and to explore the reasons why they are so special to those who do them.

The mythological dimension

Myths are strange things. They are generally found in the form of stories, but they are more than just tales. Sometimes they are expressed in poetry, or in proverbial sayings, or even in jokes. In religion they serve several purposes. They can be used for teaching, or for generating excitement, or for creating an atmosphere, or to answer questions, or to challenge and discipline people. They are very versatile, and of great importance. All religions seem to have them, though some have more than others. They can be about real people, or about imaginary characters such as gods or ghosts. They can be about actual historical events (such as floods and earthquakes), or they can be completely fictitious. The value of a religious myth does not lie in whether what it describes really happened, but in whether or not it performs its function. How it is used is often more important than what it actually says.

Myths usually become the shared property of a group or community. For example, most families have their own, and these are passed on from one generation to another, probably changing very considerably in the process of transmission. What starts out as a straightforward narrative can turn into something quite different. Because religious communities are like extended families, they also preserve and perpetuate many myths, often embodying them in their sacred writings.

This dimension of myth has always been recognised as central to religious teaching. Indeed, this is one reason why in the past so much emphasis has been placed upon the telling of religious stories. But the difficulty has always been that of knowing how to use them properly, and of choosing the most appropriate time to introduce them. When used in the wrong context or at the wrong time they do not work, and sometimes they can actually be damaging to children's understanding. This was a major point to which Ronald Goldman drew attention in the mid-1960s, when he researched into children's religious understanding.

Teachers who are unaccustomed to dealing with religious stories and myths are strongly advised to make use of reliable guide books before presenting them to children, even when preparing to tell such traditional and familiar narratives as Noah's Ark. What looks innocent enough on the surface can be full of hidden problems. The story of Noah, for instance, is not really about water, or boats, or animals, though these features come into the general tale. It is about God's response to human wickedness. It is contained in the law-books of the Jewish and Christian faiths, because it was intended to bring home the message that God will not tolerate wrongdoing. To use the myth in a completely different way, or in a different context, is to spoil it, and to invite misunderstanding. It is not a suitable story to use in RE with young children, a point which has been made by educationists for a very long time. It is unsuitable, not because it is not a good story (which in fact it is, in terms of dramatic effect), but because it implants in the children's minds the idea that God is a vengeful tyrant, who is quite prepared to drown people if he dislikes their behaviour. There are many recorded cases of young children having nightmares after hearing this story, and of others who have been upset by the thought of all the animals who failed to get a place of safety on the ark. The problem lies not with the story itself, but with the impression of God which it undoubtedly can leave in children's minds. It is much better to reserve this particular story, and certain others like it, until the children are able to appreciate what kind of tale it really is, even if this means breaking with long-standing tradition!

Once the true nature of religious mythology has been understood, two things are likely to follow. First, the teacher will probably become much more cautious when choosing which stories can safely be used, and second, it will become evident that there is a wealth of similar mythological material outside the Bible which can be employed in the service of RE. Some of Aesop's fables, for example, can be used to illustrate what a parable is. The story of Pinocchio is an excellent example of a religious allegory. With older children, the writings of C.S. Lewis can be helpful in exploring symbolism in stories.

The doctrinal dimension

Doctrines are basically teachings. They are the things which the religious community believes. In some ways they can link up with rituals and myths, because, as we have just noted, these are included among the ways in which beliefs are expressed and communicated. But the most distinctive feature of doctrines is their directness. They are often formal statements, set in the shape of creeds; they can also take the form of arguments. Again, they might be like directives, issued by a religious leader who is laying down the articles of belief which all members of the community are required to accept.

Doctrines tend to come into play on particular occasions, such as when the members of the community need to defend themselves against criticism, or when they wish to persuade others to join them. In early Christianity, for example, doctrines were formulated when the church began to spread across the world and was in danger of losing sight of its first principles. Clearly-formulated teachings helped new Christians to stay on the rails of orthodoxy; in fact, the word 'orthodox' itself means 'correct doctrine'.

Learning to recite doctrines has always been an important feature in religious education within faith communities, even at an age when the teachings could not be fully understood. But it is no longer a characteristic of contemporary RE in state schools. However, there is no reason to exclude doctrine as such from the content of RE, because if children were never given any idea of what people actually believe, then their religious understanding would be seriously impaired. The important thing is to make a clear distinction between looking at religious doctrines and indoctrinating, which is a very different matter!

The ethical dimension

Somewhere in religious systems there is likely to be a code of ethics, that is, a set of guidelines or rules intended to show the kind of life-style appropriate to the beliefs which are held. A glance at the letters of St Paul to local Christian congregations, in the New Testament, will show how he always made a point of linking religious principles with everyday behaviour. We must say at once that rules about behaviour are by no means confined to religious communities; all human societies, whether they are religious or not, have rules which determine what is acceptable behaviour and what is not. The difference between religious ethical teachings and those which are purely secular is that in the former case the foundation is to be found in the idea of what God is like, while in the latter the rules tend to be based upon ideas of what is good for the ordered running of the community.

Ethical guidelines and moral codes in religion are generally to be found within the sacred scriptures, and it is this which gives them their special authority. They are perceived as having a supernatural origin, which puts them beyond question. In some religious traditions the rules are spelled out in close detail, while in others they take the form of general principles, leaving the individual to work out how they should be applied in particular circumstances. This sometimes leaves a great deal of room for disagreement, so that it is not always very clear what the community as a whole does lay down in terms of ethical requirements. Within Christianity, for instance, there is no hard and fast rule about such things as whether it is right to kill, or to go to war; some Christians take one view, and others take the opposite. Even at quite an early stage in their education, children can be introduced to the complexities of making such judgements, not on the basis of abstract conceptualising, but through exploration of real-life situations which reflect caring, sharing, loving, and helping. This is far more valuable than learning the Ten Commandments by heart, leaving no room for personal decision-making.

The social dimension

Religions almost always find their clearest expression in the form of communities of people. It is extremely unusual to find a genuine religion which centres on only one person, although of course there can be individual ways of looking at a community faith. In some of these communities it is actually the 'togetherness' which is the main characteristic. In Islam, for example, the idea of togetherness through brotherhood pervades almost everything that is done. Beliefs are expressed in a single statement which is so simple that everyone can give assent to it. Prayers are said when everyone is facing the same way (towards Mecca) and speaking in the same special language (Arabic). In the great Pilgrimage, all are expected to dress alike so as to erase social differences. In these and many other ways, the idea of a unified community is emphasised.

Christianity, too, lays much stress upon 'oneness', and in modern times this has come to the fore in the ecumenical movement, which tries to bring together the divided branches of Christendom 'that all may be one'.

Religions are therefore social organisations of a special sort. And, as with all organisations, there are teachings about how someone becomes a member of the group, about how leaders are to be chosen, about where their authority lies, and so on. These organisations have a corporate life, which goes beyond the life-styles of the individual members. In the classroom, children can profitably explore what goes on within a religious community, and what it means to belong to this kind of family or fellowship of faith.

Because religions are communities, much of what they do, and indeed much of what they possess, has to be set in that special context. To separate out particular aspects in order to look at them more closely can often be very misleading, because by detaching them from their community setting they can lose their true nature. For example, a collection of money taken up during a service of worship is a part of the ritual, and in that context it has a special meaning; but to look at the business of collecting money on its own can make it appear quite different, because it has been stripped of its religious significance. In just the same way, the Bible has a scriptural nature and purpose within the Christian community, which sets it apart from all other books; but when it is lifted out and examined as a collection of ancient literature, it can lose that special nature and become nothing more than a set of old documents. Teachers need to be aware of what happens to religious artefacts and other phenomena when they are taken out of their social context, because it is their place within it that makes them what they are.

The experiential dimension

The last of the six dimensions of religion to which Ninian Smart drew attention is the most difficult of all to describe. It has to do with what we might call inner knowledge or experience, and often goes completely beyond the limits of ordinary language. To talk about it we frequently find that we have to resort to poetry, metaphor, art, drama or music. Whereas in the case of doctrines it is the intellect which plays the major part, in the experiential aspect of religion we are in the realm of feelings and emotions. Ninian Smart saw this as the starting point of much religious awareness, the moment when 'something happened', something in itself almost inexplicable, but setting in motion a whole series of reactions and responses. He used as an illustration the story of the Buddha in India, sitting beneath the famous Tree of Enlightenment and realising that he had hit upon the solution to his problem about the meaning of human experience. We could equally well cite instances of men and women being 'converted', or being inwardly sure that they had been singled out for some special religious vocation. The great Methodist pioneer John Wesley wrote about feeling his heart 'strangely warmed'.

We do not need here to enter into a detailed consideration of the psychological aspects of all this, but it is important for the teacher to keep in mind the fact that religion is not concerned exclusively with the business of agreeing or disagreeing with certain teachings. It has much to do with the heart, as well as with the head – with experience as well as with explanation. If children are to gain an all-round awareness of what religion entails, opportunities need to be found to 'stir' them, to develop and encourage a sense of awe and wonder, so that they can learn how to respond to what is beautiful and worthwhile. It is at this level that we begin to touch upon what worship really is. It is also here that children's curiosity starts to be aroused, as fascination and excitement lead them into fresh discoveries. It hardly needs to be added that this, in the final analysis, is what education is all about.

In our later chapter on the business of planning an RE programme we shall see how this wider view of the nature and content of RE can be brought more clearly into focus in the classroom situation, in terms of lesson material and its presentation. But enough has been said here to demonstrate the importance of showing children that religion encompasses a very wide range of human ideas, attitudes, customs and beliefs, and that a proper appreciation of it is gained only when all of its aspects (dimensions) are explored. To limit attention to only one or two of them, and to leave the rest untouched, is to make the overall picture unbalanced and therefore inaccurate.

CHAPTER 6

RE AND THE REST OF THE CURRICULUM

What is the relation between RE and the other subject areas which make up the normal primary school curriculum? Does it stand apart from them in splendid isolation, or do they interlink? More urgently, perhaps, how does RE relate to those subjects which come into the category of the National Curriculum? Does RE have its own special content, and if so, what is it? These are all important questions, not only for understanding the theory of RE but also for actual classroom planning.

As far as the relation between RE and the National Curriculum subjects is concerned, we have already observed in Chapter 2 that the law makes RE compulsory, and that Local Education Authorities have the right to set out their own attainment targets; this places RE in much the same position as the subject areas within the National Curriculum, but technically it is distinct from them. It cannot be sacrificed in order to make room for other curriculum activities, and must appear on the timetable for all pupils in the school, except those whose parents have requested that they be withdrawn. In practice, therefore, classroom planning must embrace RE, and it follows that every opportunity ought to be taken to 'marry' it to other areas in the interests of economy of time and resources. This can only be done, however, where there is a clear awareness of how it relates to these areas. This chapter offers suggestions as to how that relationship might be seen, so that opportunities can be grasped to present RE in a natural partnership with everything else that goes on in the teaching programme.

A few generations ago, when almost all schools were religious foundations, the major curriculum areas served the cause of what was then called Religious Instruction. Text books were styled in a religious way, no matter what they were about. Thus children might learn the alphabet by reciting 'A is for Angel, B is for Bible, C is for Christ, D is for Devil', and so on. Mathematics books followed the same custom: 'King Solomon had 1000 wives and 10 000 concubines. Divide the number of concubines by the number of wives.' Needless to say, this approach is no longer adopted, and today RE does not dominate the rest of the curriculum, but has to take its place as a partner within it. But this leaves us with the problem of determining what kind of a partnership it is to be.

RE and spiritual development

It is often said that the special purpose of RE within the curriculum is to cater for children's spiritual development, and that it is this particular responsibility which distinguishes it from the other subject areas. Unfortunately it is by no means clear what is meant by this statement. There are two distinct ways in which the term 'spiritual development' is commonly employed, and both of them raise serious difficulties.

The first way is to think of spiritual development as having to do with the growth of the child's 'spirit' or 'soul'. This idea derives largely from the belief that every human being is made up of three constituent parts – the physical body, the mind, and the spirit. On this assumption, certain areas of the curriculum are intended to work on one or more of these parts – physical education looking after the body, mathematics developing the mind, and of course RE specialising in feeding the spirit. This kind of theory is no longer tenable. Contemporary psychology lays great emphasis upon seeing the person as a whole, and not as a collection of different parts fastened together. The three-fold division just described is entirely artificial, as also is this way of seeing the purpose of the curriculum. Furthermore, the idea that everyone has an inner spirit is itself based on a particular religious viewpoint, and therefore begs one of the very questions with which RE is actually concerned.

The second way of understanding spiritual development is to think in terms of a 'spiritual dimension' of human experience. On this principle, RE would be concerned with enabling children to enter into a sphere of reality which is somehow different from ordinary life because it is 'beyond' it or 'above' it. To put this view in somewhat crude terms, it suggests that RE deals with another world, while all the other curriculum areas deal with this one. Once again we can see that this is an interpretation of reality which not everyone holds. It is essentially a religious view, and as such cannot be unquestioningly employed as a basic premise for educational theory.

RE is concerned with ordinary things

RE has as its content precisely the same raw material as all the other areas of the curriculum. It explores the same territory, and frequently makes use of the same tools in order to do so. Religious people do not live in a different world; they inhabit this one like everyone else has to do, and the questions which they ask are about the same sphere of reality. What is different, however, is the nature of those questions. If science asks 'How does this work?', and if art asks questions about shape, colour, form and texture, and if language asks questions about the communication of ideas, then religious education asks about the underlying significance of things. Its most probing questions are about *meaning*. Religion is a response to normal experience, based upon an interpretation of what that experience signifies. Admittedly, sometimes it does appear to go off into another world, with speculations about such matters as life after death; but these speculations are always based upon experience of the here-and-now. The subject-matter of RE is no different from that of any other curriculum area. Certain features of ordinary life do raise more obvious religious issues than others, but that is no different from saying that particular features of the landscape offer more than others to the artist or the poet. In terms of selecting the content of RE for classroom use, it means that the teacher does not have to look for something which is inherently 'religious' to teach about; rather, it is a matter of taking ordinary things and looking at them from a religious standpoint. The significance of this will become more apparent when we turn in a later chapter to RE within a topic-based methodology.

RE, then, looks at the same world and the same phenomena as do all the other classroom subjects: but it does have a closer affinity with some curriculum areas than with others, and consequently can be more naturally linked with them. We can single these out for more detailed discussion.

RE and history

People have always tried to understand history, and to draw meaning out of it. It is natural to want to make sense of the past. Certain religions, such as Judaism and Christianity, take history very seriously indeed, claiming that it is in the events of the past that God can be most clearly perceived. From historical happenings, religious thinkers in these traditions have drawn conclusions about where history is going, and they began to envisage the future by reference to the past. There is therefore a rich field of enquiry here for RE to cultivate. The historian is interested in discovering what happened in the past, but that is as far as he may legitimately go as a historian. He uses such specialised skills as archaeology to search for evidence of how things used to be, and tries to reconstruct the past from the clues that he finds.

But this is where the historian has to stop. Religion, however, goes further. It is concerned with the question of whether there is any lasting significance in the things that history shows us. Does it *mean* anything? Does it teach any lessons for the present and the future? To take an example, in the Old Testament we find what looks like a summary of the history of the Hebrew people, and indeed it does provide historians with valuable information. But it is not really history in the modern sense. It is essentially an interpretation of past events, seen through the eyes of people who firmly believed that they were watching God at work. History, to them, was not what one theologian described as 'one damn thing after another'; it was the unfolding of God's purpose, through the medium of ordinary events. Their reason for recording their history was not to build up archives, but to extract and express their understanding of God's purpose for mankind. History was the stage upon which the divine drama was being enacted.

When this important distinction is properly understood, it becomes easier to see how RE and history can work together within the school curriculum. Alongside the task of finding out about what happened in the past (which is pure history), the teacher can encourage the children to give thought to whether the past teaches us anything of value for today. Are there any clues in the past which point towards the future? Does experience (our own and other people's) teach us anything at all, or is it true that 'it's no good crying over spilt milk'? Does history seem to be going anywhere, and does there seem to be any kind of control over it? Do we make our own destiny, or are we caught in the grip of 'luck' or 'fate'? It is when questions like these are raised that genuine RE is taking place. Obviously some of them are much too sophisticated for young children, but there are others which can be asked at a simpler level. If the questions stop short at asking only 'what happened?', then that is history alone. If the children can go on to ask 'Was there a purpose behind it?', then they have moved into the arena of RE.

An exploration of almost any of the world's major religions will reveal how people have used the memory of the past to build up an understanding of the meaning of life. For example, they have devised creation myths, intended to show why the world is like it is and what part mankind has to play within it. These myths look like history, but they are not factual accounts of the past. They are attempts to expose the inner purpose of what is going on, and it is this which associates them with religion rather than history.

RE and language

Language is the medium through which people communicate with one another. It is employed for many purposes – to share ideas, to inform, to describe and therefore to understand, to direct, and even to entertain. It provides a way of organising thoughts into a coherent pattern. It has a wide range of uses. Certain activities have a tendency to create their own languages, as has become very evident in this technological age, and religion is no exception to this; there is such a thing as religious language. The meaning of the language is determined by the special uses to which it is put, and sometimes words can mean one thing in one context and something quite different in another.

When children explore the area which we call 'religion', they are actually looking at something which has a great deal to do with language and communication. Many rites and customs are really ways of saying something, ways of expressing beliefs or feelings. They are a kind of language. They frequently contain complex symbolism which has to be 'read' in order to be understood. It is one of the saddest commentaries upon contemporary society that so few people are really able to appreciate what these symbols mean, with the result that they are religiously illiterate; this is in itself one of the strongest reasons for developing RE work in this particular direction.

If teaching language to children is the business of making them literate and articulate, then we can begin to see how it links with RE. Having learned how to read, speak and write, they then have to move on to the much more important matter of knowing what to write and talk about. Language is a means to an end, not an end in itself: fluency is useless if one is talking rubbish. There must be something to be said, something which matters and is worth saying. There must be meaning in the words, and as we have said, and will constantly repeat as this book unfolds, religion and 'meaning' go hand in hand. It is no accident that in several of the world's major religions, the most profound description that can be given to something is to call it 'God's Word'. For Christians, this is a title applied to Jesus himself. For Muslims, the Holy Book (the Qur'an) is thought of in this way. Reverence for something which has been 'said' epitomises the idea that language can in itself be sacred, because it provides a bridge between man and God. Children can begin to appreciate what this means by discovering how important the Arabic language has become for Muslims, or the Hebrew language for Jews. In Christianity, for some Roman Catholics the Latin language is still regarded as being somehow more 'holy' than their everyday speech forms.

By recognising the element of language within religion, children can gradually come to appreciate what it is about. They will see that it enables people to 'speak to God' (prayers, hymns, etc.), and that it also provides a way in which God can speak to them (scriptures, sacraments, traditions, etc.). What we are seeing is that the development of language skills with children is a means of providing them with the tools that are needed for exploring the nature of religion. Through language, sometimes of a specialised kind, religious ideas are expressed and shared. The community aspect of a religion, which we discussed earlier, depends upon the ability of the members to communicate with one another.

RE and art

It almost goes without saying that a great deal of the world's finest art has been prompted by religious feelings. A visit to any place of worship will illustrate the extent to which art forms are used as expressions of religious devotion. Buildings have been designed and erected to the glory of God. Beautiful manuscripts have been produced, especially in Christianity and Islam, as ways of showing reverence for the sacred scriptures. Stained glass windows often serve a variety of purposes – to commemorate, to teach, or to beautify. Producing a work of art is often thought of as being in itself an act of religious devotion. Even with very young children, an exploration of the world of art can stimulate feelings of wonder and awe, and as we have seen, this is among the aims of RE. To be able to recognise what is beautiful, and to distinguish it from what is ugly and worthless, is itself a religious skill. Within the general term 'art' we can, of course, include music, literature and drama, which all offer immense teaching potential for work in RE.

RE and science

The relation between RE and science has for a long time been a source of controversy. There are still many people who imagine that the two are mutually contradictory, with science offering one explanation of reality, and religion offering another which stands in direct opposition to it. The Biblical story about Adam and Eve is often cited as if it were an alternative to Charles Darwin's theory about how mankind evolved, and teachers have even been heard to tell children that the Bible story is what Christians believe, while the theory of evolution is what scientists believe.

Frankly, this is nonsense. It is based upon a mixture of ignorance and misunderstanding, with more than a smattering of the religious illiteracy to which we drew attention above. The word 'science' refers to the scientific method of looking at things, which came into its own during the nineteenth century as an approach to examining the world around us. To look at something 'scientifically' is to examine it objectively and dispassionately. It is to sift the evidence and make judgements based upon careful analysis of the facts obtained through testing procedures. It is essentially neutral in character, and if the scientist becomes emotionally involved, or for any reason allows his feelings or prejudices to influence his findings, then he ceases to be a true scientist.

Out of the scientific method there did arise a view that if something could not be subjected to tests in these ways, then it had no validity. It was argued that anything incapable of verification by science had no reality. But it then became clear that this in itself was not a very scientific thing to say, since there was no way of proving it. The argument cut the ground from under its own feet.

Today the dust has largely settled after what was certainly a serious and heated period of controversy. It has now generally been acknowledged that science and religion do not necessarily stand in opposition to one another. Indeed, science is now commonly applied in religious studies. Most serious scholars in the world of religion employ such sciences as archaeology, textual research and linguistics as tools for exploring the formation and meaning of religious traditions. It is out of the development of science that there arose the contemporary 'critical' approach to the study of religion. This approach involves looking at the beliefs, documents and customs in their widest context. Who wrote the books of the Bible? In what languages were they written? Where was the writer living at the time, and what was going on when he wrote? To whom was he addressing his words? These are all historical and scientific questions, and the answers to them provide the evidence upon which objective judgements can be made.

When children are 'doing science' in the classroom they are actually developing their critical faculties. They are learning how things work, and how to make them work. They are discovering how to sift evidence and draw legitimate conclusions from what they find – how to be objective rather than subjective in their decision-making. The skills and attitudes which they acquire in doing this can be employed when they are exploring religion, and this is precisely what the contemporary 'open' approach to RE is all about. When a child discovers that the earth is round, and that it revolves around the sun, and that gravity has to do with the attraction of one body for another, then he or she is gathering together the facts or data which will equip him or her to make an informed judgement about the world we live in. Those facts, in due course, will prompt the child to ask fundamentally religious questions. Is there an overriding pattern to all this? Is there evidence that it has any purpose? How should human beings treat this incredibly complex universe? Does it all raise any moral questions? Do the discoveries which science makes possible lead us away from religion, or do they in fact compel us to stand in awe and wonder at the greatness of it all? What does it do to our understanding of the value and nature of human beings?

As far as the primary school classroom is concerned, it is important that the teacher should see how the development of children's scientific skills can enrich their ability to explore all aspects of their environment and their experience. It is not a matter of searching for ways of bringing RE into play in science work, but rather of understanding how these differing aspects of the curriculum interrelate and contribute to one another, even when, for practical purposes, they may be taught quite separately.

Other curriculum areas

The curriculum areas discussed above are those which have the closest affinity to RE, and which can most readily be linked with it. There are, of course, other things that go on in the normal school day. Some would want, perhaps, to claim that PE should be mentioned (along with health education) on the ground that many religions regard the body as a 'temple' in which God is glorified. This idea can be found in the thought of St Paul (see I Corinthians, 3:16). But there are other faiths which treat the human body quite differently, almost despising it as something which hinders true spirituality. In certain Indian religious traditions, for example, the body is severely disciplined to the point of self-mutilation. So we cannot claim that it is a *universal* religious duty to respect the body: but what we can say is that in some religions (notably the Jewish–Christian tradition), there has always been emphasis laid upon regarding the body as the instrument through which God is either obeyed or disobeyed. Immoral or careless use of the body (one's own or someone else's) has always been thought of as religiously unacceptable, and spiritual health has been regarded as closely linked with bodily fitness. The avoidance of those things which abuse the body (such as drugs, excessive eating and drinking, self-indulgence, etc.) has long been regarded as part of a Christian's proper life-style. While it would be going too far to claim that PE and health education are extensions of RE, nevertheless there are occasions when children can be helped to see the important connection between belief and physical behaviour.

RE and moral education

Strictly speaking, moral education is not part of the school curriculum as such, though there have been many voices raised in support of the idea of making it a formalised lesson activity. It has often been thought that this is where RE makes its most important contribution, and parents have been heard to say that, in their view, RE is important because 'it teaches children the difference between right and wrong'. Yet it is now widely agreed that everything that goes on within the school ought to be seen as contributing to the children's moral development. The structure of the school as a whole, with its rules about conduct, will obviously help. So also will the attitudes of individual teachers, through the degree to which they demonstrate fairness, kindness and general professional integrity. RE does not carry the sole or even the main responsibility for children's moral growth.

But it is also acknowledged that religion and morality do have much in common. Virtually all the major religions of the world contain moral codes within their teachings (see Chapter 5) and a clear connection is made between what people believe and how they behave. So, while affirming that RE is not to be regarded as identical to moral education, at the same time it does have something to say on the matter. One cannot teach about any religion without making reference to its moral or ethical codes. What is special about the contribution of RE is that it shows how, for many people, the ultimate foundation for all moral conduct lies in religious rather than pragmatic principles. Rules about right and wrong are bound up with concepts of what God is like, rather than being founded upon theories of human rights or upon rational argument. Some of the lesson outlines in Chapter 11 illustrate possible approaches to the moral dimension of RE with children of different ages.

There is no reason why the teacher should not from time to time give the children an opportunity to reflect, as part of their RE work, upon the other things that they do in school, as a way of giving coherence to the curriculum. Why are they learning these particular things, and why do they learn in these ways? By asking the question 'Why are we learning?', all sorts of opportunities can be raised and grasped for dealing with matters of meaning and purpose. This is what true RE is about – taking time to stand back and consider everyday experience. In this sense, RE brings the whole of the curriculum together, and when this is properly done it exposes the true relationship between its diverse parts.

B
PLANNING AN RE PROGRAMME

In this section, practical guidance is given concerning the actual putting together of a programme of RE across the whole school. The following are discussed:

▶ the topic approach and its value

▶ the process of planning a whole-school RE programme

▶ examples of RE programmes for infants and juniors.

CHAPTER 7

THE TOPIC APPROACH

In primary schools, where the class teacher has responsibility for most, if not all of the curriculum areas, two basic approaches are possible. One is to structure the learning on the basis of separate subjects, allocating a fixed amount of time for each: the other is to adopt the topic approach, in which a theme or centre of interest is chosen; this is then explored from a variety of curriculum directions, extracting mathematics, language, science, history, etc. as they arise naturally out of the selected theme. Sometimes a third approach is adopted, which is really a combination of these: the topic method provides the main bulk of the work, and what does not arise easily out of it is then added as a kind of supplementary teaching, perhaps in the form of a mini-topic running alongside the mainstream work. It is quite common to find this happening, particularly in the case of such lessons as swimming or PE, where teachers find difficulty in making natural links with the chosen centre of interest. A variation of this has come to be known as the 'drills and frills' approach, the drills being the traditional disciplines such as handwriting, spelling, mathematics tables and reading practice, and the frills being the topic work. These are sometimes split up so that the drills occupy the morning, and the frills are reserved for the afternoon. It used to be almost universally assumed that all RE (especially when it was called Scripture) would be in the category of supplementary teaching, since, on the surface at least, it did not appear to lend itself to inclusion in the topic approach, and this is still common today. The view taken here is that in fact RE *can* be embraced within most topics in a perfectly natural way, and that where it cannot, there is no reason why it should not form a separate theme on its own.

There is no such thing as the right approach. What works for some would not succeed for others, because circumstances differ and so do teachers. But it is clear that the topic approach has commended itself very widely across the country as a whole, so much so that in some areas it has actually become the official policy of the Local Education Authority, and schools in such areas are required to adopt this method of working.

Certainly the topic approach does have much to commend it, especially in the atmosphere of the National Curriculum, where teachers are being pushed more and more towards planning their work on the basis of whole-school topics in order to find time for all they are expected to do, and to show how progression can be monitored. We can set out the main advantages, over against the disadvantages, in the following brief summary.

The advantages of the topic approach

1 It encourages and facilitates joint activity, both at the planning stage (between the teachers) and at the learning stage (between the children as they work together in a co-operative way).

2 It helps to develop learning skills ('learning how to learn'), because the children are able to come to the chosen topic in their own ways.
3 It exposes the interrelation and interdependence of the various subject areas, thus giving the children a clearer awareness of how each discipline contributes to the processes of discovery and understanding.
4 It is closer to the kind of learning that goes on naturally outside the confines of the school. Real life does not present itself in neat compartments labelled 'history', 'art' or 'mathematics', but is experienced all in one piece and then approached from different directions.
5 In these days when there are so many things that have to be covered under the umbrella of the National Curriculum, it can facilitate economy of time by providing a single focus for a variety of activities.

The disadvantages of the topic approach

1 If not managed carefully, the topic method of teaching can quickly become artificially contrived, and the chosen area of interest can turn into little more than a pretext.
2 An unsuitable topic can severely limit learning opportunities, and can actually lock out some curriculum areas altogether.
3 Enthusiasm for one area of the curriculum while engaged upon the topic can lead to the neglect of others, producing unbalanced learning.
4 Heavy demands can be made upon the teacher's management skills if the topic is to work effectively.
5 If insufficient thought is given to the choice of topics, the result can be a piecemeal and arbitrary programme of work, lacking coherence or progression.

The disadvantages are not insuperable. Careful consideration of the initial topic choice will go a long way towards overcoming most of them, and in any case no topic should be allowed to turn into a chain which binds the teacher to a particular way of working. As we have observed, there is no reason why, from time to time, other work should not be introduced quite separately from the central focus of interest. The advantages of the topic approach, however, are very great indeed, and far outweigh the occasional difficulties. It is for this reason that, throughout this book, the topic method is advocated, and the suggestions offered are in line with this approach.

However, it should not be thought that this book is consequently of no use to teachers who are not working according to the topic method, and are instead structuring their work on the basis of separate units or subject areas. The examples of possible RE work can easily be lifted out from their topic context and treated as free-standing blocks of lesson content. However, even the staunchest advocate of the 'separate lesson' method would probably agree that there has to be *some* sort of continuity running through the individual teaching sessions. This is usually achieved by following a progressive programme, in much the same style as was characteristic of early Agreed Syllabuses. These, as we have seen, took the Bible as their basic platform (their 'topic'), and the development was largely found in adopting a chronological approach ('the history of God's people'). This meant that each lesson was not in reality free-standing at all, but followed on from what had gone before, and prepared the way for what was to come next. In other words, the newer topic approach is not really very different from the separate-subject method, except insofar as it focuses upon a selected theme rather than upon a more general area.

Criteria for choosing suitable topics

Ideally, all topics should be selected not only for their inherent interest, but also for their potential in developing as many as possible of the major curriculum areas. Naturally some are more suitable than others in this respect. For example, the topic of dinosaurs can be absorbingly interesting, and can produce valuable learning opportunities in history or science or art or language work; but it will do precious little for RE, unless the teacher distorts it beyond recognition or (worse still) distorts RE itself. If the RE work is to be successful, and if it is to be treated as a real element within the total curriculum, then it must be kept in mind when the choice of topic is being made. The teacher should ask 'Can I develop RE work out of this topic?', and if the answer is 'No', then consideration should be given to whether it ought to be set aside in favour of one which is more suitable. If there are overriding reasons why that particular topic ought to be chosen, then the RE work should carry on separately alongside it, and not just be left out altogether. Furthermore, when the RE value of a topic is under consideration, thought should be given to the extent to which it can expose the children to as many as possible of the 'dimensions' of religion to which attention was drawn in Chapter 5, and to whether it can meet the broad range of aims and objectives which were set out in Chapter 3.

It may be useful here to identify some topics which do lend themselves to wide application across the curriculum, including RE, in a natural way. These should be viewed only as selected examples and not as an exhaustive list. There are many others which could be added, and no doubt teachers will wish to extend the range for themselves. All of those identified below are *general* topics, out of which RE can legitimately be drawn. They are not RE topics in themselves.

Topics for younger primary children [key stage 1]

Myself	Food
Homes	Shape and colour
Friends and neighbours	Growing
People who help us	Big and little
Caring and sharing	Light and dark
Seeing and hearing	Happiness is . . .

Topics for older primary children [key stage 2]

Families	Strong and weak
Journeys	Signs and symbols
Books	Rules and regulations
Communication	Buildings
Special days	Beginnings and endings
If only . . .	Patterns

Every one of these topics, when examined closely, will be seen to have potential in a variety of ways, and this exemplifies one of the main criteria for choosing a topic that can be used in developing RE. We can set these criteria out in the form of a checklist of questions to be asked, as follows.

Criteria for choosing a topic for RE

1 Can it embrace most, if not all of the main curriculum areas, in a natural way?
2 Is it within the range of the child's experience, so that he or she can recognise elements within it, identify with them, and thus contribute to what is being learned?
3 Does it permit the teacher to be flexible in his or her approach?
4 Does it invite, in a natural way, exploration from the standpoint of RE, meeting a variety of the basic aims and ranging across the various dimensions of religion?
5 Can it readily be tailored to fit the amount of time available to the teacher, by extending or contracting the amount of content?
6 Can it be presented at different levels, to meet the needs of children of varying abilities and backgrounds?

Some of the above topics, and certain others, can be seen more fully worked out in the lesson examples in Chapter 11; but it will be through testing them in the actual classroom situation that the teacher will best be able to judge their usefulness.

THE PLANNING PROCESS: A SEQUENCE

In recent Agreed Syllabuses there has been a movement away from the earlier prescriptive approach towards a style which gives teachers freedom to devise their own programmes of work. This freedom has, to some degree, always been inherent in syllabuses; it was assumed from the beginning that teachers would be selective in what they presented to their pupils. But that freedom has now been extended, and in some cases it has actually been transformed into a responsibility. Take, for example, the Essex Agreed Syllabus *Building Into the Future* (1987): the section entitled 'Syllabus' is only four and a half pages in length, and is made up entirely of general principles and aims for various age levels. It concludes by saying that

> **"** . . . the intention of the Essex Agreed Syllabus for Religious Education is to give schools a framework within which to construct their own specific teaching programmes. **"**

Building into the Future (Collins, 1987)

This freedom to plan the work in a way which is best suited to one's own school situation has been generally welcomed, but at the same time it has placed a heavy burden upon the shoulders of teachers who have no expertise in this area of the curriculum. This chapter, therefore, offers guidelines for putting such an RE programme together, within the constraints of what the law, the LEA's Agreed Syllabus, and the pressures of the total curriculum demand.

Who does the planning?

The requirements of the National Curriculum have brought teachers face to face with the realisation that they must plan on a long-term rather than a short-term basis, and that the construction of programmes of work must now be done through corporate thinking across the whole school. The days have largely gone when a teacher was able to shut her classroom door and then 'do her own thing', regardless of what was going on among her colleagues. One outcome of this has been the acceleration of the trend towards identifying a member of the teaching staff who will accept overall responsibility for a particular area of the curriculum, and thus become the subject co-ordinator within the school. This has for some time been a practice in the case of particular subjects such as mathematics or science, but it is only in recent times that it has been extended to RE.

It is, without doubt, a practice to be commended: but care needs to be taken in choosing a teacher who really does understand what is involved. Unfortunately it has often been the case that someone has been identified on questionable grounds ('You go to church, don't you?'), reflecting the low status that RE has been accorded in many schools.

It is one of the responsibilities of this member of staff to keep abreast of current thinking in the field of RE, and to share his or her insights with colleagues by using staff development days, or through the dissemination of occasional literature, book reviews and notices. But the major responsibility would be to act as a co-ordinator for whole-school RE programme planning.

The advantages of whole-school planning in RE

The advantages of devising a whole-school RE programme are very considerable, for example:

- ▶ It can embrace a broader spectrum of aims and objectives.

- ▶ It can offer a more balanced diet of learning.

- ▶ It can reduce the risk of repetition.

- ▶ It will bring teachers together for planning, thus introducing a greater range of ideas and experience.

- ▶ It encourages clearer focusing upon issues of direction and purpose, because it provides a bird's-eye view of where the work is leading.

- ▶ It lends itself to more accurate and effective monitoring of the children's progress.

- ▶ It can be integrated into the whole-school planning for the core National Curriculum subjects.

Such planning cannot, however, start from scratch. The groundplan will be set out in the Local Education Authority's Agreed Syllabus, which must by law be the foundation for all RE in state-maintained schools. It is there that the teachers will find the fundamental principles and aims, usually supplemented by more detailed guidance on how these can be put into practice. Some authorities publish handbooks or sets of resource materials for use in their own areas, and it will be from these that the initial inspiration is drawn.

But there will still be a great deal of further work to do, and if the LEA has also taken up the option to set its own attainment targets in RE, then these too will have to figure in the preliminary planning processes. A set of outline attainment targets can be found in Chapter 13. What each school must do is to match these mandatory prescriptions to its own local situation, working out a plan which will extend right across the school, and will also demonstrate adequate coverage of all that the Agreed Syllabus demands.

The planning sequence

There is a natural sequence of steps to be taken in programme planning, and in the case of RE there are particular points which have to be kept in mind. We can examine each of these steps in turn, and then set them out at the end of the chapter in the form of a simple diagram which can serve as a checklist.

Step 1: Rehearse basic aims

All planning starts from an understanding of aims and objectives. We have already discussed these (see Chapter 3), but now is an appropriate point for the teacher to look at them again. To see them set out in a formalised way is helpful in ensuring that all of them, or as many of them as possible, are catered for at some stage in the body of the programme. This is also the proper point at which to refer to the LEA's Agreed Syllabus. It is likely to contain not only a summary of the basic aims of RE as they are perceived by the Authority, but also a general guide to the suitability of particular material for any given age range. There may even be examples of worked out programmes for the teacher to follow, with suggestions for resources. This is how the Agreed Syllabus was meant to be used. And, as we have already noted, any RE attainment targets which the LEA may have set should also be studied at this juncture, because they, too, will need to be taken into account when planning the work to be covered.

Step 2: Assess teaching circumstances

Before any actual topics or lesson content can be decided upon, thought has to be given to the circumstances in which the teaching will be carried out. Obviously this will include a professional assessment of the ability levels with each class – something which every teacher takes into account when planning any part of the curriculum: but in the case of RE there will be certain other relevant issues to consider. For example, is the school set in an 'all-white' area, where there are no children from ethnic minority groups? If so, then it may be that greater emphasis is needed upon a multi-faith and multi-cultural content, in order to compensate for the fact that the children are lacking direct and regular encounter with people of non-Christian faiths. Or, alternatively, is the school one in which there is a strong or even a majority representation of other religious traditions? If this is the case, then the RE programme will have to be planned so as to take this into account.

A further issue is what can be known about the children's backgrounds, as far as their experience of religion is concerned. In short, what do they know already, which might provide the starting point for developing their understanding and experience? No longer can it be assumed that all of them have been inside a place of worship, either on a regular basis or even infrequently. Not all of them will have been baptised. Some may have attended a wedding, but most will not. Close association with a religious community is no longer the norm, as it used to be, and because of this many children have a blank spot where in earlier generations their religious background would have been. A student teacher recently reported that, after telling her class of junior children the story of Christmas, one boy asked 'What was the baby's name again, Miss?'

Finding out what children already know about religion can be a delicate business. At all costs, teachers must not give the impression that they are probing into the family's religious background, because this is bordering upon illegality, and will almost certainly bring protests from parents. It is far better to sound out the children in an impersonal way, perhaps through a quiz or in general class discussion.

A common question arises about what to do when there are known to be children in the class whose parents will withdraw them from RE; these children are usually Jehovah's Witnesses, but other religious groups are also involved. Should the RE planning be adjusted so as to take such children into account? The answer, quite simply, is 'No'. Technically, children who are withdrawn from RE are regarded as being out of the class for that particular area of the curriculum and the teacher's responsibility for teaching them is removed. Planning the RE work should therefore go ahead in the normal way, and not be curtailed or modified to suit those who will not in any case be taking part.

Finally in this respect, all RE planning has to be carried out with an eye on the calendar. This is because throughout the year there are festivals and special days which cannot be ignored, and need to be embodied within the programme. The obvious examples for Christianity are Christmas and Easter, but the special days of other religions are also important, especially to those who observe them. These external constraints affect RE in particular, and do not affect other curriculum areas in the same way; indeed, the major Christian festivals so dominate the school activities that at those particular times they become the central topics around which most of the classroom work is planned.

Step 3: Agree main topics

This is the point when all the members of staff come together to hammer out the overall work throughout the school, under the direction of the headteacher. Because this planning has to cover the entire curriculum, with particular emphasis being laid upon the National Curriculum subjects, it will almost certainly be a fairly lengthy process, involving more than one meeting. It will be the task of the RE co-ordinator to ensure that the interests of RE are taken fully into account, either by proposing topics that are themselves explicitly religious (such as 'Churches' or 'Festivals'), or by trying to ensure that the general topics being put forward are capable of serious development in RE. The essential questions to be asked are those which are set out in Chapter 7.

Sometimes it will be the case that major topics do not naturally lend themselves to RE work, or that they cannot be used for the particular aims and objectives that are necessary at that stage. Where this happens, it is perfectly legitimate to identify what might be called mini-topics which meet the specific needs of RE, and to include them in the teaching programme as independent units of work. Provided that this does not become the normal practice, it does no harm at all. The trouble only begins when *all* RE work is treated in this way, and the children are given the impression that RE is always distinct from everything else. This will certainly be the case unless every effort is made to integrate RE into the mainstream topics, by choosing those which make this possible.

To summarise so far, then, we can say that at the whole-school planning sessions, topics of two sorts will eventually be agreed: there will be those which are broadly-based and capable of including RE aspects in a natural way, and there will be occasional separate or discrete mini-topics, which will cater for the RE work when it cannot easily be drawn out of the major themes.

A completed whole-school RE programme is likely to be in the form of a calendar or diary into which these two kinds of topics have been slotted. In the case of the major topics, what will appear in the programme will be the title of that topic, with the specific RE element entered beneath it, clearly identifying the particular aspects or units of work which will develop the children's religious understanding. In those places where the major topic did not lend itself to RE work, there will be an independent RE mini-topic, capable of standing on its own. In terms of the actual appearance of the programme, these will look much the same; the only noticeable difference will be that some topic titles look more explicitly 'religious' than others. Figure 8.1 gives an example of a possible junior RE programme. An infant programme would look very similar, but with broader topics which reflect the approach adopted with younger children. In the interests of clarity, only one topic has been identified for each term of the school year, but it is recognised that many schools prefer to operate on the basis of half-termly rather than termly centres of interest. In these cases there would be two topics entered, where, in Figure 8.1, only one appears.

Figure 8.1   An example of a junior RE programme

YEAR 3	YEAR 4	YEAR 5	YEAR 6
Term 1 *Beginnings* Birth/naming Christmas	Term 1 *Special people* Muhammad/Jesus Christmas	Term 1 *Celebrations* Hannukah/Christmas around the world	Term 1 *Rules and laws* Religious laws and duties
Term 2 *Light and colour* Colours with a meaning	Term 2 *Books* Sacred books The Bible	Term 2 *New life* Despair/hope Easter	Term 2 *Power and energy* Ideas of God
Term 3 *Buildings* Places of worship	Term 3 *Communication* Stories and parables	Term 3 *Clothes* Religious dress	Term 3 *Customs* Ceremonies and rituals

Another responsibility is now laid upon the RE co-ordinator, before the next step can be taken, and that is to ensure that the RE programme has *coherence*. A danger when working with the topic approach is that it can become 'bitty', and lose its balance. As far as RE is concerned, the best way to deal with this is to look at the proposed programme in terms of the 'six dimensions' of religion which were outlined in Chapter 5. Does the programme appear to present opportunities for introducing all or most of these aspects of religion, or is it heavily weighted on one dimension at the expense of others? Furthermore, does it allow for reference to be made to a reasonable range of religious traditions, or is it limited to only one? Questions such as these will help to give the programme its final 'polish', and, of course, behind all the questions there must lie that of asking whether the proposed work contributes to furthering the overall aims and objectives of RE.

Step 4: Consider necessary resources

The most immediate resource in teaching is the teacher; but this should not be taken to imply that he or she is expected to know everything. It is natural, when planning a teaching programme, for teachers to incline towards those areas of content in which they feel confident, and to shy away from others where their background is limited. Consequently the unfamiliar subject matter of RE is always likely to be at risk of being left untouched, unless the teacher can fill the gaps in his or her knowledge. Nowadays that can readily be done, because there is much easier access to information than was the case in the past. Most Local Education Authorities have set up RE resources centres which are within reach of the schools in their areas, and similar facilities are also to be found under the auspices of churches and other religious bodies. Some are within teacher-training establishments, where they serve the needs both of the students and the teachers in the locality. Such places ought to be the teacher's first port of call in RE programme planning, because they can offer a kind of lifebelt to those who fear that they may be in danger of sinking. Books, artefacts, videos, project boxes, wallcharts and a host of other things can either be borrowed or inspected, and advice is often given to meet individual needs. The later discussion of resources (see Chapter 18) makes some practical suggestions about building up resources within the school, and identifies some particularly useful materials.

It is worth repeating that the pressures created by the demands of the National Curriculum have highlighted the importance of seeing *time* as a resource. Programme planning must take account of how this precious time is to be allocated between the various subject areas. Official guidelines have made it clear that central government will not prescribe exactly how much time ought to be spent on particular aspects of the curriculum, but it is expected that pupils will be allowed sufficient of it to undertake worthwhile study. A few minutes on a Friday afternoon will not be adequate, and the RE co-ordinator may have to underline this point at planning meetings within the school.

Step 5: Consider evaluation procedures

The issue of evaluation and assessment in RE is a particularly difficult one, and requires a more detailed consideration than is possible in this chapter. This is given in Chapter 13. For the moment, however, we can say that even in the early stages of programme planning and preparation, some initial thought should be given to how the programme might best be evaluated when it reaches its conclusion. Obviously there will be a close relationship between the initial aims and the final retrospective analysis, since the former will establish the goals and the latter will determine whether they have been reached.

Figure 8.2   The planning sequence: a checklist

STEP 1	Rehearse basic aims and objectives in RE, against the background of the Agreed Syllabus and any locally agreed attainment targets
STEP 2	Assess teaching circumstances – environment, children's background and previous experience – check calendar
STEP 3	Agree curriculum topics at whole-school level, with RE co-ordinator checking that the needs of RE are being met, and contributing possible topic ideas
STEP 4	Consider necessary resources, including allocation of time, against background of National Curriculum requirements
STEP 5	Keep evaluation procedures in mind

EXAMPLES OF INFANT RE PROGRAMMES

The following pages contain two examples of one-year RE programmes – the first for younger infants (ages four to five) and the second for older infants (ages six to seven). Each is put together on the basis of the topic approach, but it would be a simple matter to adapt them to other ways of teaching, for instance by using selected areas from the programmes as independent units of work.

Each example is first set out in the form of a simple diagram, sub-divided into three termly sections, with a basic topic web suggested for each term. The topic web itself contains what is considered to be a realistic number of strands; to add more would not be difficult, but it would be impossible to cover all of them in a single term. The text following each diagram explains and expands what the webs contain. The work suggested is, of course, matched to the aims set out in Chapter 3.

Two points need to be clarified. First, these are examples of the *RE element only*; it is left to the teacher to add suitable extensions to the web so as to cater for the other areas of the curriculum. These are not 'RE topics', but illustrations of how RE can be drawn out of a general centre of interest.

The second point is that these are examples of long-term programmes, so the degree of detailed content is at this stage only minimal. Chapter 11 provides more specific ideas about how these general areas can be filled out, by selecting one theme from each of the topic webs and suggesting possible lesson approaches.

Notes on RE programme for younger infants (Reception/Year 1)

General

With very young children, RE is virtually indistinguishable from the rest of the curriculum, and in reality takes the form of what has come to be known as 'pre-religious education'. At this stage the child's most pressing need is to establish himself or herself in a world which is at the same time both fascinating and frightening. Before children can embark upon formal learning they must be helped to feel secure, and to know that they matter. Here and there a few tentative steps in recognisable RE can be taken, but they will be very basic indeed, and largely identical to those which the child has to take in order to establish himself in the general learning environment.

Figure 9.1 Example of a one-year RE programme: infants (Reception/Year 1)

TERM 1

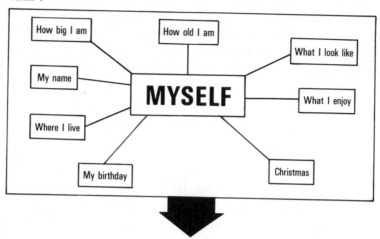

TERM 2

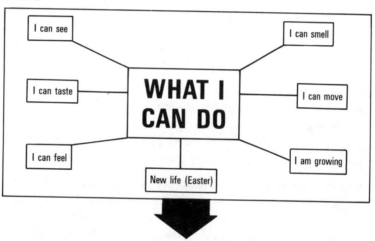

TERM 3

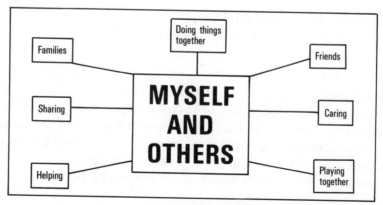

For this age group, there are three immediate realities. There is their own selfhood; there is their increasing awareness of what they can do; and there are the people around them, whose lives impinge most directly upon theirs. Before they can reach out into the wider world of experience, they must come to terms with these realities. They must find out about themselves, each working out their own identity and their own characteristics. They must find out what they are capable of doing; and they must begin to work out the nature of their relationships with others. These things are the beginning of all learning, and they are also at the heart of all religious enquiry.

Term 1

Here, the central theme of the work is 'Myself'. The general aim is to provide opportunities for the child to build a foundation of self-awareness and self-confidence, an aim which, of course, is shared with all the other classroom activities at this early stage. To be able to recognise one's own name, and to respond when others use it, may seem a very elementary skill: but if a child cannot do this, then he or she cannot develop very far as a person. Children start to learn how to differentiate between themselves and others, and how to recognise what belongs to them and what does not. They establish their fixed points – their home address, their physical appearance, their own personal experiences, and their likes and dislikes. In short, they begin to appreciate the fact that they are persons, that they each have a unique identity, and that they matter.

Basic as this may seem to be, it is really an early approach towards answering the fundamentally religious question 'Who am I?' Children can explore their own personal characteristics – how old they are, how tall they are, and the colour of their eyes and hair. Skin tones can be considered, and if the class contains children from ethnic minority groups, a start can be made in giving them (and the others) a sense of pride in their own distinctive appearance.

The work can be extended into an exploration of birthdays and how they are celebrated. Since the topic as a whole is directed towards developing the concept of self, birthdays are a particularly appropriate theme because they are in fact 'self-centred'. All children, of all cultures, seem to acknowledge birthdays, with the notable exception of Jehovah's Witnesses, but these will in all probability be withdrawn from formal RE work in any case. Furthermore, the birthday work moves naturally into the Christmas theme, which will be topical during this term. The children will want to share experiences of what happens in their own homes, and here we have a valuable way of laying foundations for later exploration of religious customs, celebrations, and special days.

The evaluation of this term's work will be a matter of assessing the extent to which the child has settled and integrated into the school community, and how well he or she is relating to others. The degree to which a child participates in such activities as news-sharing and groupwork will provide clues to this. There should also be some first signs that they are developing attitudes of curiosity and inquisitiveness, and that they are capable of responding to new discoveries inside and outside the classroom. If a child has a sense of wonder, and is at the same time showing a respectful awareness of the rights of the other children in the group, then progress clearly has been made.

Term 2

The work in RE suggested for this term continues and extends what was contained in the previous plan. Again, the main aim is still that of developing self-awareness and of fostering a sense of enjoyment, but to this is added the further intention to develop some of the basic skills which will be needed in the ongoing learning process. If the children actually enjoy finding out, then they have the key to self-motivation and eventual autonomy. They will want to probe more and more deeply into their increasingly varied experiences, and here again we encounter another of the characteristics of genuine RE (see aim 8 in Chapter 3).

Simple work on the human senses can start here, though of course it will not be exhausted for a long time to come. It points the child in the general direction of all the curriculum areas, including RE. The senses are brought very much into play in all religious traditions. Colours, images, shapes, smells, sounds, textures and tastes all contribute enormously to the world of religious experience. Later, children will be able to find out how the things that they see, hear, touch, taste and smell can all be meaningful, but if they are to do that, they must start here.

As this term progresses the first signs of spring will be appearing, and no doubt the teacher will wish to capitalise on this fact. The theme 'What I can do' lends itself to this, because the emerging colours and sounds in nature can be drawn into classroom work. The fact that the child himself is growing (both in size and in capability) can be linked to the more general fact of growth and change in nature. To observe how seeds come through the soil, having been planted by the children themselves, will help to awaken their sense of wonder and achievement. It is doubtful whether the teacher ought to start introducing ideas about God being behind nature, because that would be to pre-empt the children's own questions. The issue of where life comes from can be left open until the time when they are ready to explore it more fully.

The arrival of spring affords an opportunity to make links with the Christian festival of Easter. Despite what is sometimes said to the contrary, there is a genuine connection between the two in terms of meaning. Admittedly there are certain aspects of Easter celebrations (such as chocolate eggs and Easter brides) which have no proper place in the religious traditions, but the idea of life following death certainly is one of the main themes of the festival, and this can be hinted at in work related to the new life which is evident in spring, after the seeming deadness of winter.

It is true that Easter is a difficult topic to approach with very young children, but if the emphasis is placed upon the happy side (new beginnings), it can be explored without distortion, leaving the more sombre side to be considered when the children are older. Stories about precious things being lost and then found again can be used without straying too far from the meaning of the Easter festival.

Again, evaluation of the term's work will be a matter of determining whether the initial aims have been achieved. Is the child becoming more independent? Is he now starting to ask questions out of genuine curiosity? Is he becoming more aware of his environment, and of himself within it? If the answers to questions of this kind are 'Yes', then the programme has been worthwhile.

Term 3

In the third term the main thrust of the programme is towards the building up of relationships. The aim now is to encourage children to look away from themselves and to start to identify the nature of their social encounters. Although they are still very egocentric, an introduction can be made to the development of their social skills. There are fundamentally two things that they need to learn: they must discover how other people relate to them, and how they in turn can respond. So they must consciously recognise the importance of these people who share the world with them, and the various roles that they play. In terms of RE, this is the commencement of work directed at developing their sensitivity towards those who are different from themselves. It is really the start of a multi-cultural encounter, because the children are constantly meeting new people whose appearances and life-styles are diverse. It is also an important step along the path of moral education.

So, through the work contained in this programme, the children explore first of all the relationships within the group that each knows best – the family. They work out what a family is, and who belongs within it, including themselves. They identify those who are their friends, and think about what friendship actually involves. Through reference to their own experience, and through a variety of activities and stories, they come to see what sharing and helping mean in concrete terms. They are not yet ready to deal with abstract concepts, but by working as members of a group or team they come to appreciate that co-operation necessarily involves give and take on all sides. Sharing equipment, sharing responsibility for decision-making, and sharing in problem-solving are all important ways into RE as well as into the general process of socialisation.

The suggested work on 'Doing things together' could include an exploration of family activities such as holidays or outings. Here again is an opportunity for the child to reflect upon special days, customs in the home, and perhaps also upon those particularly important times when the family is gathered around the meal table. The influence of television has affected this to some extent, and many families sit not around the table at all, but in front of the TV set, while balancing a tray on their laps. In other families it may be the case that all the members are rarely together to share a meal at the same time. Even so, the teacher will see that there is a link to be made here with religious customs such as the Jewish Passover, the Sabbath (Friday night) meal, and the Christian service of Holy Communion. These may not be mentioned explicitly at all, but to think about the specialness of eating together is an introduction in itself.

The principles behind the planning

In the above notes, the underlying aims have been identified, and it is worth stressing here the importance of bringing these aims to the surface when the planning begins, and setting them into the broader context of the aims and objectives listed in Chapter 3. The work suggested, even with the youngest children, can contribute usefully towards the achievement of four of the stated aims, namely:

> ► To help children to acquire and develop those skills which will enable them to appreciate religious ideas and practices (aim 2).

- To encourage attitudes of openness and sensitivity towards people whose religious beliefs and customs may be different from their own (aim 4).

- To foster a sense of awe, respect and wonder, leading to a desire to penetrate more deeply into those areas with which religion is concerned (aim 8).

- With other areas of the curriculum, to contribute towards the children's moral development (aim 9).

When we come, in Chapter 11, to look at some specific lesson examples, we shall see that other educational objectives, beyond those which relate directly to RE, can also be identified in the proposed activities.

Cautionary note

The experienced teacher will know that there can be hidden dangers in any work which involves direct reference to the children themselves and their home life. Embarrassment could be caused, either to the children or to their families, if this is not handled with sensitivity. Teachers will need to use their professional judgement and their knowledge of each child's personal circumstances if this embarrassment is to be avoided.

Notes on RE programme for older infants (Year 1/Year 2)

General

This programme starts at the point where the child has begun to move away from his or her earlier egocentric outlook and has grasped something of what it means to belong to a wider community. Among the general aims of the programme is that of further developing attitudes of openness and sensitivity towards other people, through exploring feelings and recognising that others have them too. We noted earlier that the experiential dimension of religion has to be given its due place in RE, and here is a good place to begin – through reflection upon inner feelings in general.

In the first term the children consider the nature of particular human feelings such as anger, fear and envy. In the second term they experiment with some of those feelings by trying to enter imaginatively into situations outside their own. Then, in the third term, they start to explore feelings in a different way, through concrete examples of people who engage in helping and caring, and the feelings or motives which prompt them to do so. Some of the examples suggested are very familiar (the nurse, the doctor, the policeman), but others are also included so as to broaden the child's understanding. In addition, the topic web provides an opening for the teacher to warn the child that not everyone is helpful. The danger inherent in work on this theme is that it can very easily become sentimental, leaving the child with the impression that the whole world is out there for his or her benefit. The stark truth is that some people cannot be trusted, because their intention is not to help but to harm. Parents who rightly warn their children against speaking to

Figure 9.2   Example of a one-year RE programme: infants (Year 1/Year 2)

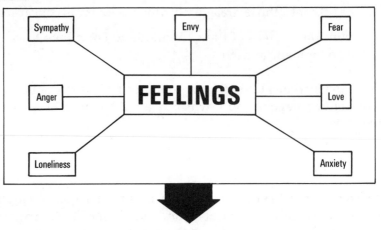

TERM 1

Sympathy

Envy

Fear

Anger

FEELINGS

Love

Loneliness

Anxiety

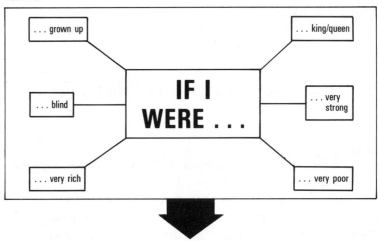

TERM 2

. . . grown up

. . . king/queen

. . . blind

IF I WERE . . .

. . . very strong

. . . very rich

. . . very poor

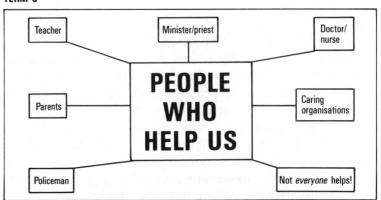

TERM 3

Teacher

Minister/priest

Doctor/ nurse

Parents

PEOPLE WHO HELP US

Caring organisations

Policeman

Not *everyone* helps!

strangers or accepting lifts from them will not thank a teacher who appears to be undermining this caution by suggesting that all people are nice.

It is also important that the teacher does not confuse genuine helpfulness with normal public services carried out by people who are merely doing their job. It is at this level that sentimentality can creep in unnoticed, and what starts out as an enquiry into people who help us turns into a succession of job descriptions. The fundamentally religious dimension emerges only when the child begins to appreciate that helpfulness demands a particular kind of unselfish motivation.

Term 1

We noted earlier that feelings play an important part in religion, and of course children experience these at a very early age, long before they are able to put those feelings into words. When a parent asks 'How much do you love me?' and gets the answer 'Twenty million' or 'A mile and a half', the reason is that the right words have not yet been discovered. But there is no doubt that the feelings are there. To begin to understand what they are, to recognise that other people have them too, and to start to reflect upon them, are all important steps forward in laying the foundations for RE.

Work on feelings will probably be in the main a matter of talking, discussing in groups, role-playing and story-telling – using material which illustrates or which actually stirs feelings within the children themselves. It is not difficult to arouse excitement, disappointment, or even a mild degree of fear among the children, but care has to be taken that it is always done within a secure and controlled context. When the children sense that they are safe they can be encouraged to talk about their own feelings (fear of the dark, fear of being lost, excitement at an imminent birthday, worry about going into hospital). Here the experience and understanding of the teacher will be called very much into play. The children will be able to write descriptively or produce art work in which they can put some of their emotions into symbolic shapes and colours. Drama is likely to play a significant part in the expression of feelings. This is an excellent, if somewhat tentative introduction to the place of feelings in religion and religious art. It also reinforces the children's awareness that other people have feelings, too.

The festival of Christmas occurs during this term, and so also do some important festivals in other religions (for example, Hannukah in Judaism). There are stories, traditions and customs associated with these festivals which are in themselves very exciting and evocative. Opportunities can be grasped to use these as part of the overall topic work, because they arise naturally out of it.

Most of the data required for evaluating this sort of programme will be embodied in the quality of the work done by the children and in an assessment of their responses to particular activities. The teacher would probably want to look for signs of developing sensitivity in the children, towards others and towards their own feelings. This can be tested in a rough and ready way by using photographs depicting facial expressions or body language which the children are invited to interpret, thus revealing their growing awareness of how to read the signs which show how other people feel.

Term 2

During the second term the focus of the programme is a development from the first. Armed with a clearer understanding of the nature and range of human emotions, the child is invited to imagine himself in a variety of roles and situations. Only a very small range has been suggested here, simply to illustrate the approach, and teachers will be able to extend this much further if desired. Once again the use of stories will be considerable, and these can be drawn from conventionally religious sources such as the Bible, or from secular literature. There is an excellent opportunity here to introduce some of the parables of Jesus, such as the Good Samaritan and the Prodigal Son, because this is precisely how these stories were meant to be used. They were told in order to stir feelings and to invite people to put themselves in other people's shoes. Stories can also be drawn from the religious and secular literature of other cultures, to introduce a broader spectrum of ideas and outlooks.

There is no need to restrict this work only to imaginary situations. News reports about people in trouble or in need, or factual information about various human experiences, can all be used to give the children a foundation of concrete reality upon which to build their role-playing.

What is intended here is not that the children shall dramatise situations with a view to performing a play in front of an audience. This is an educational activity, an exercise in empathising, as the child tries to use his imagination to get inside a situation and sense what it is like to be there.

How is this justified as real RE? Very easily, if the teacher understands the nature of religion itself. We have tried to show that religion is not just a matter of holding particular beliefs or performing particular rituals: it is a way of penetrating deeper into reality, of taking the lid off life to look inside. In this work the children are starting to identify the inner nature of human experience. Admittedly it is at a very basic level, but it is a beginning, and the foundations are being laid for what comes later.

Term 3

The topic of 'People who help us' is so well known and so widely used that it scarcely requires commentary. Yet its very familiarity can be its downfall. It is not always used to much advantage, and certainly it does not always contribute a great deal to RE. As we have already observed, what is frequently missing is the thing that matters most – the exposing of the *motives* for helping others. There is nothing particularly special about helping old ladies across the road if that is what one is being paid to do. True helpfulness is demonstrated by those who do things because they want to, and not because they have to.

Furthermore, the range of 'helpers' is often very limited. Even parents tend to be left out, as if they are supposed to help and therefore do not really count. Only occasionally does one find mention made of the local religious leader such as the vicar or the minister. The consequence is that the children have little or no idea of what his or her work involves, and would not be likely to regard that person as a source of help in times of difficulty. In a recent small-scale survey carried out among junior children, it was found that virtually none of them had any real awareness of what the local vicar, minister or priest actually does, apart from leading Sunday services and marrying people. To explore the work of people like these, including of course the leaders of other religious traditions too, would give the children a clearer insight into the nature of religious commitment. If the children have an opportunity to visit a place of worship (see Chapter 12), they could ask direct questions of the person in charge, and explore the reasons why anyone should want to enter what we usually refer to as the caring professions.

Relating the planning to the aims of RE

Once again, we have to affirm the importance of keeping the basic aims of RE in view. The topic work suggested in the above one-year programme has been chosen with the following aims in mind (see Chapter 3):

▶ To help children to acquire and develop those skills which will enable them to appreciate religious ideas and practices (aim 2).

▶ To make available factual information about religion and religious phenomena (aim 3).

▶ To encourage attitudes of openness and sensitivity towards people whose religious beliefs and customs may be different from their own (aim 4).

▶ To provide in particular an awareness of the nature and claims of the Christian religion, and of the part which it has played in shaping the cultural and social life of Britain (aim 5).

▶ To help children to identify those areas of human life and experience in which religion plays a significant part (aim 6).

▶ To explore with children the relation between religion and other areas of experience and knowledge (aim 7).

▶ With other areas of the curriculum, to contribute towards the children's moral development (aim 9).

10

EXAMPLES OF JUNIOR RE PROGRAMMES

SYMBOLS

This chapter contains two examples of possible one-year RE programmes for use with junior children. The first is for lower juniors (Years 3 and 4) and the second is for upper juniors (Years 5 and 6). They are set out in a three-termly format, with one topic suggested for each term. If the teacher is accustomed to working in half-termly topics, then that will not affect the value of the examples given, because they are illustrations only and can be adapted to suit local circumstances. They are also capable of adaptation for older or younger pupils, and for use as free-standing lessons. The notes which follow the diagrams explain the principles which lie behind them. As with the infant programmes outlined in the previous chapter, it is emphasised that the topic webs represent only the RE aspect of the broad theme chosen, and it is assumed that the teacher will expand the ideas so as to cover the other curriculum areas.

Because these are essentially programme plans and not lesson outlines, they contain very little by way of specific content. They should be viewed as the rough sketch which precedes the detailed drawing. To attempt to introduce too much detail at this stage in the planning can only serve to obscure the direction being taken. Nevertheless, the areas selected within each term's proposed work should be sufficient for the teacher to begin to focus upon possible lesson ideas and materials. Chapter 11 narrows down some of these areas, to give illustrations of what might be done in actual classroom activities.

Notes on RE programme for older infants (Year 1/Year 2)

General

Younger juniors (ages eight to nine) are generally capable of developing a theme or topic in greater depth than infants, and can sustain it for a longer period of time. In this suggested one-year programme the main aims are to provide factual information, to stimulate interest, to develop particular skills, and to increase sensitivity in the areas indicated. A considerable part of the programme is dedicated to the exploration of what it is that makes something 'special', and if time permits this can be extended into an examination of 'value' or 'worth'.

Term 1

The final term's work in the upper infant RE programme, suggested in the previous chapter, was focused upon 'People who help us', and this next topic for lower juniors forms a natural

Figure 10.1   Example of a one-year RE programme: juniors (Year 3/Year 4)

TERM 1

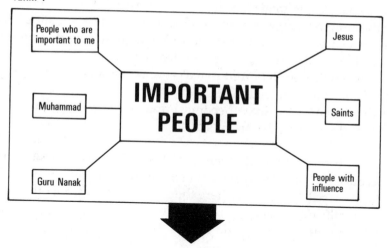

TERM 2

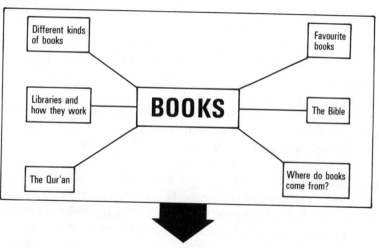

TERM 3

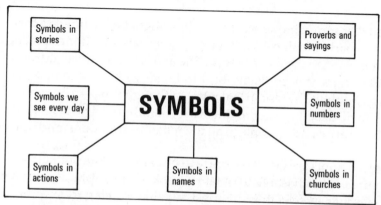

continuation from that. By thinking about the people who are most important to him or her, the child starts to explore the various ways in which someone becomes significant in the lives of others. Such special people might be close at hand, within the family group, or special friends: alternatively they might be more remote, such as television personalities or sporting heroes who have become special because they are admired. The junior child is now beginning to identify heroes and heroines, and here is an opportunity to make use of that fact for teaching purposes. The various qualities that are required to make someone special can be explored, and from that starting point the teacher can lead the enquiry into a wider field. Can the children think of any people, past or present, who have become important for their qualities of leadership, their courage, their wisdom, or their special skills?

In the proposed RE programme the names of Jesus, Muhammad and Guru Nanak have been singled out because each is at the forefront of an important religious tradition, and therefore has to be regarded as special. In schools where there are children from other faiths it may be thought appropriate to identify different personalities, and the task of making this decision will be one of the responsibilities of the teacher who knows the local situation.

Obviously these special people can be introduced only in a fairly general way, through a simple outline sketch of their life history. Doctrinal matters must be left until later. But because this is the Christmas term it will naturally be topical to focus upon Jesus in particular, and this gives the teacher an opportunity to consider the birth narratives contained in the Gospels of Matthew and Luke. It is also a chance to point out that there are similar birth stories about other great people such as Muhammad, the Buddha, and figures from Jewish history. It is an opportunity, too, for the child to see the Christmas narratives in the broader context of Jesus's whole life; one of the most common faults in teaching about Christmas is that it is treated independently of what followed, and the result is that for many children Jesus remains as the baby in the manger. He seems then to jump from infancy to crucifixion, with nothing in between.

When dealing with important religious figures, great care must be taken not to cause offence to those who belong to particular traditions. For example, Muslims are not permitted to make pictures or any other kind of image of the Prophet Muhammad, nor to portray him in dramatic presentations. So it would be improper to ask the children to draw or paint pictures of this nature, or to become involved in role-playing. Even though the Muslim children themselves may not protest, their parents certainly will.

It is suggested that some simple work on saints might be included in this term's work. This could be linked with a particular local saint if one is associated with the area, or with the saint who has given his or her name to the local church. The aim is to give the children an idea of what the word 'saint' actually means. It is probably best to begin with a contemporary or near-contemporary figure (such as Mother Theresa in Calcutta), although it has to be remembered that, technically, someone has to be dead in order to qualify for sainthood! The teacher should also keep in mind the fact that there are saintly people in all the religious traditions, and not just in Christianity.

Some recognised saints are far too obscure to be of much educational value, and others are largely legendary figures. It is advisable to obtain a book of biographical information which will act as a guide to the teacher in selecting the most suitable for classroom presentation.

Term 2

The stories of some of the special people just described can often be linked with equally special books. For example, it is in the pages of the New Testament that we find virtually all our information about Jesus. Sometimes that special book, rather than being about the special person, is thought to have been written by him, or else delivered through him to the general community. The sacred book of Islam (the Qur'an or Koran) is thought by Muslims to have been sent by God through revelations to the Prophet Muhammad. He is not thought to have written it himself, but heard it and passed on what it said. It is therefore treated as holy, and beyond criticism or question. As children investigate this they will gradually become more aware of what it is that makes a book sacred in particular religious traditions.

Junior children are becoming more competent in their use of books, and are ready to explore the wide range available. Books are not all the same, nor are they all used in the same way. Some are dictionaries, others are story books or instruction manuals or catalogues. There are books of fiction, and there are books of fact. The children will thus become conscious that books have to be approached and used in different ways. They will also discover that certain books are more important or influential than others. Here the teacher can introduce the Bible as a special book, explaining how it was put together and how it is used. The children could glance at its general structure and perhaps read a few selected passages to gain an idea of its contents. This is too soon to go into great detail, and in any case it is important for the children to develop an understanding of the *nature* of the Bible before they embark upon a more thoroughgoing exploration of what it says. As many have pointed out in the past, there are grave dangers inherent in trying to use the Bible too soon.

Term 3

The third term's work in this sample RE programme moves into the area of religious language and symbol. The study of special books in the preceding term will have prepared the way for this, because the children will have discovered that some stories are factually true and others are not. Some stories come into the category of 'tales with a meaning', and have to be interpreted rather than simply read.

This is quite a difficult area for some children to grasp, so it is suggested that the work might be introduced by looking at other kinds of symbols first of all – traffic signs, trade marks, the London underground symbol or the blue lamp outside the police station are all possibilities. They contain little or nothing in words, yet all of them have a meaning, and in their own special ways they 'say' something.

There are also symbolic actions which the children will recognise – shaking hands, bowing the head, pointing the finger, clapping hands and so on. Each is an action with a meaning, and through looking at pictures or by seeing demonstrations the children will begin to appreciate how frequently symbols are used in everyday life. Symbols can also be found in people's names, or in the names of streets, villages and towns. There are symbols in numbers (unlucky 13), and examples of these can be found in the Bible (for example, 'seventy times seven' in Matthew 18:22 means 'for ever').

The point about exploring symbols is that these play an extremely important role in religion. When people try to express their religious ideas and feelings they are sometimes lost for words, because ordinary language will not go far enough to meet their needs: so they turn to symbolic language. Ceremonies, rituals and customs are rich in symbolism, the meaning of which is commonly missed by those who have never given it much thought. The clothes worn by a bride and her bridesmaids, for example, or the vestments of a priest are all symbolic. A place of worship will usually have some kind of symbolism built into its design and its furnishings, ranging from a simple cross to much more complex shapes and images. Equally, there is symbolism in what is sometimes missing – as for instance in an Orthodox Jewish synagogue, which has no musical instruments, or in a Free church, which has no altar.

Work of this nature is of tremendous value in developing the child's religious awareness and understanding. It can begin at a very basic level. A good introduction is to utilise old Christmas cards by asking the children to identify the designs which say something about the meaning of Christmas, contrasted with those that do not. Here again we see a way of probing beneath the surface or outward appearance, something which, as we have noted already, lies at the very heart of all religious enquiry.

Programme aims

With the child's increasing age and capability it is possible for the teacher to attempt a greater number of aims. In the lower junior RE programme described above, virtually all of the basic aims outlined in Chapter 3 can be touched upon, some at a more ambitious level than others, for example:

▶ To provide factual information about religion to the pupils (aim 3).

▶ To further the acquisition and development of skills (aim 2). The work on symbols in the third term will be of considerable value here.

▶ To encourage attitudes of openness towards different religious beliefs (aim 4).

Notes on RE programme for older juniors (Year 5/Year 6)

General

The typical upper junior child is more questioning than he or she was a year or two earlier, and less ready to swallow everything whole. Children of this age want to know why things are as they are, and why they should do as they are told. They are more capable of making their own choices and decisions, even if these are not always in accord with what others expect of them, and they are acquiring a set of criteria for doing this. They still need the approval of their peers, and they will often allow their personal judgements and standards to be suppressed in order to remain accepted members of the group; but they are recognising that there are reasons behind the routine which they are expected to follow, and that the ultimate seat of authority is not necessarily the teacher. To a considerable extent they can now work out for themselves whether a thing is 'right'

Figure 10.2   Example of a one-year RE programme: juniors (Year 5/Year 6)

TERM 1

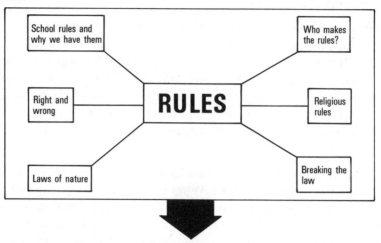

TERM 2

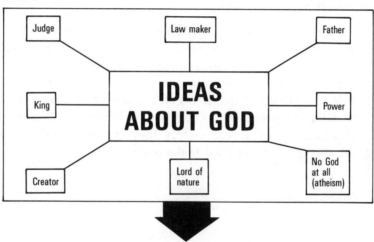

TERM 3

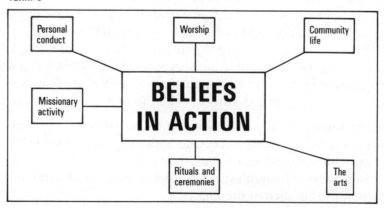

or 'wrong', though they still need help in some of the more complex situations. They are becoming more analytical, and are starting to seek a reasoned and valid justification for the things that they are being asked to do.

This programme of RE work begins, then, at this point. In the first term it raises some of the issues relating to social and anti-social behaviour, asking questions about the ordinary rules and conventions with which the child has become familiar. It encourages him or her to explore the reasons why there have to be rules in any ordered society, and to ask who makes them. Linked with this are the basic questions of morals and ethics, no longer at the simple level of authoritarian instruction, but rather in terms of 'Why should I?'. Religious laws and 'natural laws' are included within the scope of the enquiry, as also are issues relating to what is likely to happen when laws are broken.

In the second term the work is developed into a simple exploration of ideas about the nature of God as the ultimate authority figure. What exactly do people mean when they speak about 'God'? What sort of concept comes to mind? Various distinctive analogies are presented, and the children are invited to consider the nature and force of each. Honesty will compel the teacher to include reference to the fact that many people do not believe in the existence of God at all, and even at this stage pupils are not too young to think seriously about this. The opportunities for a multi-faith approach here are obvious.

In the third term, it is suggested that the pupils look more closely at some of the ways in which people's beliefs about God, and about the meaning of life itself, are given expression. These will be revealed in the rituals of worship, in art forms (including literature), in personal life-styles, and in social or community life. There is more than a little truth in the old saying that actions speak louder than words, and a study of religious behaviour is an effective way of entering into the more sophisticated field of religious belief. As yet, these children are still too young to take this very far. They must wait a year or two longer before they can start to put some of these ideas into a coherent pattern. But they can at least make a start.

Term 1

Rules and codes of conduct are found in all societies. They are experienced on a small scale within the family group, and on a large scale they spread across all communities and cultures. No group can function without rules. The children can start to investigate this by considering the basic school rules (keeping to the right or left, not running in the corridors, keeping to time, treating property with respect, maintaining order, etc.), and then by suggesting others. The value lies not merely in rehearsing the rules, but in appreciating why they exist. From this there can develop a study of how rules are made, and by whom. Here we enter into questions of authority which, in a more complex way, are part and parcel of the life of all religious institutions.

Within religions there are different kinds of rules. Some relate to moral behaviour (how to treat one's fellow human being), some have to do with the proper ways of worshipping God (rituals), and some deal with correctness of belief (orthodoxy). There are rules about rank and status within the community (hierarchies). Each kind of rule could form an area of enquiry in itself, depending upon the abilities of the children.

As an element within this term's work the pupils might give thought to what are generally called 'laws of nature', the kind that are not man-made. This is a point at which religion and science can begin to interact upon one another. There is scope, too, for exploring basic questions of what happens when laws are broken. Here is an opportunity to consider such concepts as justice, punishment and mercy, though careful preparation would be necessary for such work to be effective at this level.

Term 2

In the second term the children are introduced to some of the ways in which people think and talk about God. What is God supposed to be like? Is it even possible to give a description? What sort of characteristics would God be likely to have? What ideas come to mind when the word 'God' is used? Are there any right answers? This is the stage at which the teacher can help the pupils to break free of the notion that God is an old man in the sky, wearing long clothes and sporting a beard. Various images and symbols could be taken from some of the world's religions, and the children should be given an opportunity to consider the possibility that God may not exist at all. Simple arguments for and against the existence of God could produce valuable discussion.

Pictorial art, poetry, stories and music can all be drawn into this particular exploration; many hymns contain word-pictures of God, which the children could discuss. Famous prayers, too, expose beliefs about God's nature (judge, father, creator, etc.). This kind of work also helps to extend the children's vocabulary, as they encounter and learn to use unfamiliar terms.

Term 3

The work suggested for the third term is really an extension from the previous two. It comprises in the main an exploration of how people's religious beliefs affect their lives. This can be explored at two levels – the personal and the social. *Personal conduct* is affected by what people believe to be right or wrong, and *social behaviour* is evidenced in such things as corporate worship, community-based religious activities, and so on. Uniformed organisations attached to churches, organised charitable work such as Christian Aid or TEAR Fund, all illustrate things that people do together in the social context of religious life. A religious community is one in which people demonstrate both the personal and the social effects of their religious beliefs, so a study of what goes on within a Christian church or a Jewish synagogue could be of great value here.

Some religions (though by no means all) are committed to the principle of spreading their message to others, so that missionary work becomes a major activity. The two main religions which do this are Christianity and Islam. Judaism does not undertake this kind of work, because of its view that God has already chosen those whom he wants as his special people. The children can find out what modern missionaries do. Most missionary organisations and religious denominations will provide information about this, and details of some of their addresses will be found in Chapter 17.

Religious belief also stimulates another kind of behaviour – it prompts people to produce works of art to express their devotion. Music, paintings, sculptures, drama and literature (including poetry) are all areas for exploration in this context. In Islam it is considered wrong to make pictures of people, so Islamic art has tended to develop in a different direction, finding expression in calligraphy, pottery and ceramics, weaving and carpet-making. The making of intricate geometrical patterns is a special feature of this particular faith, not merely for decorative purposes but as a way of worshipping God.

Certain religious ceremonies could be regarded as art forms in themselves, because many of them embody dramatic features or involve the wearing of symbolic clothing. Naming ceremonies and initiation rites enshrine ideas about God or about the meaning of life, and in the hands of an informed and sensitive teacher these can all be fascinating areas of exploration.

Planning aims

In this suggested programme, every one of the aims set out in Chapter 3 will at some point be furthered, either explicitly or implicitly. It will be obvious that, particularly during the first two terms, emphasis is laid upon encouraging the children to *consider* specific issues, thus giving them practice in developing the skill of thinking religiously, something that will prove to be of crucial importance later on. Factual information will also be provided through class discussions and through research, and this is rather more evident in the third term's work (aim 3).

Note

The topics suggested here are now becoming more detailed than they were in the earlier programmes, reflecting the growing capabilities of the pupils. Heavier demands are thus likely to be made upon the teacher's personal knowledge. There will be more information to be communicated, and the differences in the children's ability levels will become more evident, thus creating problems of a different kind. The provision of reference materials in the classroom, to which both the teacher and the children can turn, will become of greater importance, and in this respect the RE Resources Centre and the local religious communities are likely to be of help.

C

PUTTING IT INTO PRACTICE

This section shows how the RE programme can be filled out with lesson content, giving advice on classroom approaches to particular topics. It covers:

▶ suggested lesson ideas

▶ practicalities and opportunities when visiting a place of worship

▶ assessment and evaluation in RE.

CHAPTER 11

IMPLEMENTING THE PROGRAMME

In Section B we considered how best to approach the task of planning an RE programme, and four examples of one-year schemes were suggested. We now come to the business of identifying actual lesson content, to fill out the general areas indicated. The comments which accompanied each example pointed in particular directions, but obviously more is needed if the programmes are to be of practical value.

Because each of the programmes contained about 20 possible themes, plainly we cannot develop every one of them here; so what the reader will find in the following pages is a selection taken from each of the four age-related diagrams, once again to illustrate teaching approaches and content. Ideas are offered concerning factual information, how it might be presented, and what the children might do. Resources are identified in Chapter 18.

It almost goes without saying that teachers are strongly encouraged to be as creative and original as they can with what is suggested here; no claim is made that the approach suggested is the best or the only one possible, and what would work in one place could be a complete failure somewhere else.

The amount of time available for each of these activities will depend upon local circumstances; teachers will be able to judge for this themselves when they see what the lesson outline involves, and set it against their other curriculum needs.

At the beginning of each lesson outline, the main aims and objectives are indicated in a way which links them clearly with the general aims of RE as set out in Chapter 3.

Lesson outline 1: infants (Reception/Year 1)

Theme of activity 'My birthday'

Objectives

- ► To encourage reflection on the experience of celebrating
- ► To give practice in language skills through talking and listening
- ► To find out how others celebrate a special day, thereby helping to develop an awareness of, and sensitivity towards different ways of doing things.

The work can be introduced through questioning the children – who has just had a birthday or will be having one soon, or has anyone in the family had a birthday? What is a birthday for? It is a time when people remember the day on which they were born. On our birthday we count ourselves as being one year older. We cannot remember the day of our own birth; sometimes our parents or other people tell us about what happened.

Out of this kind of questioning and discussion is drawn a basic understanding of what a birthday really is – an important start in the children's learning because many of them do not actually realise that it has anything to do with the day they were born. It is a way of marking our progress through life. Just as we mark distances to see how far we have travelled, so we mark points in time to see how old we are. This could, if desired, be linked with telling the time.

How do we celebrate a birthday? Different people do different things. In our country it is usual to receive gifts from members of the family and from friends. Sometimes we have a special treat, such as going out on a visit. Many people like to have a party, inviting their best friends as well as members of the family. We receive cards to wish us a happy birthday, and we put them around the room where everyone can see them. Sometimes we have a badge to wear, which says something like 'I am 5 today'. If our birthday comes on a day when we are in school, perhaps the other children sing 'Happy Birthday' to us, in the classroom or during the assembly.

Does anyone have a birthday which they share with someone else – a brother or a sister? Are there any twins or even triplets in the class? How do they feel about sharing a birthday? Is it better, or not so nice? Does anyone have a birthday which comes on a day which is already special, such as Christmas Day? What happens then? How is it celebrated? What about those people who have a birthday on 29 February?

The children can look at pictures of birthday celebrations and pick out a) the things which they themselves do at home; b) the things which are different from their own celebrations. Art work can be done, when the children paint or crayon pictures representing what they think are the best things about birthdays. These might include the birthday cake, with the appropriate number of candles on it, or a picture in which colours have been carefully chosen to symbolise a happy time ('What do you think are "happy" colours?').

Because the children are so young, at this stage it is impossible to range very widely; but by doing the things suggested here they are beginning to recognise what a celebration is, what the giving and receiving of presents signify, and what it means to have friends and families. They will gradually become aware that people do not always celebrate in exactly the same way. By choosing appropriate colours for their art work they are taking their first steps into the world of symbolism, which is itself a significant feature of religion. In addition they are exploring what is familiar, as a first step towards reaching out into the unfamiliar – the essence of all learning.

As resource material the teacher will no doubt wish to use suitable stories about birthday celebrations, and these are not difficult to find. A warning is given, however, against searching through the Bible to find a birthday story which is thought to give the work its 'religious' character. The lesson as it stands is already contributing to the child's religious development. In any case, there are only two Bible stories about birthdays, and both are totally unsuitable!

Lesson outline 2: infants (Reception/Year 1)

Theme of activity 'I can see'

Objectives

▶ To create an awareness of the gift of sight

▶ To develop an appreciation of the world of shape, light, and colour

▶ To help the children to become sensitive towards those whose sight is impaired

▶ To develop understanding of the importance of seeing, looking and observing, leading eventually to the arousing of curiosity and an enquiring attitude.

A short game of 'I Spy' could introduce this work, with the teacher drawing specific points out of it afterwards: we need our eyes to see things around us; sometimes we have to look harder, because things are occasionally overlooked; why are some things easier to see than others? – because they are bigger, or brighter, or nearer. Things are still there, even if we fail to see them. How do we know what they are? We recognise them by their shape, their colour, their size; but sometimes we need to use our other senses too, just to check that our eyes are not making a mistake.

How could we manage if we couldn't see? Short games could be played, such as 'Blind Man's Buff', or the children could try to recognise one another when blindfolded. The game of pinning the tail on the donkey will reinforce many of the points being made – we sometimes 'feel' our way when we can't see.

If time allows, some basic and very simple work could be done looking through a magnifying glass or a telescope, for the children to discover detail which cannot be seen with the naked eye. Reference might also be made (but tactfully, so as to avoid embarrassment!) to the wearing of spectacles as an enhancement of seeing.

The work can develop by asking the children to describe things which they saw on their way to school, or in the playground, or while they were on holiday. Why do they remember those things in particular? Sorting items out by colour is also helpful, because none of the other senses can be brought into play, so seeing is recognised as of crucial importance. Are there any coloured things that help us when we see them? Red lights tell us where there is danger, and green lights tell us that it is safe to go. A short mime game could be played, in which the children have to draw all their information from what they see.

In work of this kind, several important things are being learned which contribute both to RE and to the rest of the curriculum. The children are beginning to appreciate consciously that sight is precious. They are becoming aware of how to use their eyes purposefully, so that seeing becomes a learning skill. We find out about things by looking at them. We also communicate and recognise by seeing. There are many things that we would not be able to do at all if we could not see. The children are also beginning to develop feelings of empathy towards those who have impaired vision, and are learning how to 'stand in someone else's shoes'. It is through the refinement of the use of sight that skills of perception start to be polished.

Once again, it is quite unnecessary to hunt through the pages of the Bible to find stories about people having their sight restored, in order to give the lesson a religious slant. Such stories are too sophisticated for the children to understand, and in any case they add nothing of value to what has been done. The RE is already implicit in the activities suggested, and one is tempted to add, 'if the teacher can see it'!

Lesson outline 3: infants (Reception/Year 1)

Theme of activity 'Families'

Objectives

▶ To begin to develop the children's awareness of the wider community around them

▶ To increase understanding of what a family is, and of what it means to belong to a family

▶ To show the children that there are many kinds of families, and that they themselves may belong to more than one.

Religious communities, whether they are Christian, Muslim, Sikh or anything else, generally think of themselves as being like family groups. They have a head of the family in the shape of a priest or minister or imam. They have a central meeting place, which they look upon as being like their home. There is a sense of caring among the members, and they help and support one another. They eat together, and often these meals have a very special significance. In some groups, such as monastic orders, it is usual for the members to refer to one another by family names such as 'Father', 'Mother', 'Sister' and 'Brother'.

Furthermore, family language is often used when thinking about God. In both the Jewish and Christian traditions God is commonly referred to as 'Father' (though this is never the case in Islam). Conversely, those who belong to the religious community think of themselves as being like God's children.

In the light of this, any work which the children can undertake to extend their awareness of what a family is will at the same time be sowing the seeds of understanding about religious communities, even though it may not yet be apparent.

The work might be introduced by asking the children to put some particular items (such as coloured blocks, shapes or pictures) into 'families'. The word 'sets' could be used, but the term 'family' needs to be stressed in order to make the point more obvious. Why do these things go together? Because they look alike, or because they have some other feature in common with one another. They share something. The likenesses can then be identified, until the children appreciate that a 'family' is a kind of unit in itself.

They can then go on to think about human families, extending outwards to include grandparents, uncles, aunts, and cousins. Do the members have to live in the same house in order to be members of the same family? Do they have to look alike, or can they still be members of the family

69

even when they are different? What do the children think goes on within a family? Here, of course, care has to be taken to avoid embarrassing any children whose family life might be insecure, but this is something that only the teacher can know. Stories about family life, illustrating particular important aspects, will be invaluable, as also will reference to any current television series which reflects home life in some way. This should not be restricted to families living in Britain, or to those which reflect traditional British life-styles; here is an opportunity to think in multi-cultural terms.

Questions about sharing, helping, taking responsibility and so on will all arise naturally out of this work. If the children produce pictures of a family at home, the teacher could look for hints of stereotyping. Are the women and girls always portrayed as washing up or cleaning, while the men and boys are engaged in more interesting and exciting activities? Is Mummy always doing things around the house while Daddy 'goes to work'? Such images can be identified and discussed, even at this early stage.

Thought can be given to matters of decision-making in the family group. Who chooses which television programmes everyone will watch? Is there any discussion at home about the colour of the wallpaper or the name for the new kitten? Although this may appear trivial, it opens up to the children the fact that in any human group there are things that have to be done together, and that sharing is a matter of give and take. With careful handling, even the subject of family arguments can be explored, to illustrate the fact that sometimes it is not easy to reach agreement. Loyalty to the family is another important aspect for consideration, though it will not yet be something which the children can articulate very clearly.

Family customs, traditions, in-jokes, oft-repeated stories and treasured family possessions can all be talked about, the point being that religious 'families' have exactly the same kinds of things too. Religious communities develop ways of doing things in common. They venerate particular members, they pass down traditions, they collect and treasure special objects, just like ordinary households. Thus, when the children are thinking about what a family is, they are at the same time learning about what a religious community is, even if they do not yet realise it.

Lesson outline 4: infants (Year 1/Year 2)

Theme of activity 'Fear'

Objectives

▶ To explore the basic human experience of fear, as something to be understood

▶ To help the children to appreciate that everyone experiences fear

▶ To show the positive aspects of fear

▶ To introduce the idea of 'awe' at a basic level.

The theme of fear has been suggested as an element within a broader topic on 'Feelings', and it is important that it should not be treated in isolation. Young children need opportunities to identify, recognise and reflect upon their emotions, so that gradually they might learn to exercise control over them. Fear is probably the most important of all at this stage, because the child is small and therefore vulnerable. His greatest need is for security, and fear is what people experience when that security disappears.

The work could be introduced by inviting ideas about the things that make people afraid. At first there will probably be some generalised responses, but as they gain in confidence the children will become less inhibited and start to express their feelings more openly. Fear of the dark, fear of being lost, fear of water, or heights, or spiders – these and many other suggestions are likely to emerge as the discussion proceeds. No doubt the teacher will also be able to offer personal contributions, and this will give the children even greater confidence when they see that adults have similar feelings to their own.

Stories which have an element of fear and mystery within them can be used to stimulate further ideas. The teacher may find that the boys are less forthcoming than the girls, because of the notion that they are supposed to be tough, and that fear is a sign of weakness. This will have to be worked out very carefully, especially if someone reveals a particular fear which others do not share.

The positive side of fear can then be considered. It helps to stop us from getting into dangerous situations. If we are afraid of heights, then we do not climb. Fear makes people cautious. Someone who is totally fearless could also be utterly reckless; examples could be given of people who have done silly things (such as playing 'Chicken' on railway lines) to prove their bravery. This is an excellent opportunity for the teacher to press home the lessons of safety.

How do we deal with fear? We find a safe place. What sort of a place would that be? Somewhere familiar, somewhere close to someone we know and trust, somewhere strong and secure. Another way is to find out as much as we can about the thing that we are afraid of, because when we understand it better it might not be so terrifying. Fear is often the result of ignorance or misunderstanding. Thunder and lightning are less frightening when we understand what they are. Fear of snakes, or mice, or spiders, can be overcome by finding out more about them and even handling them. In the same way, fear of doing something we have never done before (like starting school or visiting the dentist) is overcome by actually doing it and finding out what it is really like.

Because this theme takes the children into the realm of feelings rather than facts, the most appropriate activities will take the form of generating those feelings and finding ways of expressing them. So the emphasis will be upon stories, pictures and videos, talking and discussing together, making pictures, and acting. Gradually it should emerge that the children's common experiences and shared feelings help to draw them together, as they start to recognise something of themselves in others. They will also become less afraid of their own natural emotions.

Handled with sensitivity, this kind of work contributes to that special aim in RE which deals with the fostering of a sense of awe, wonder and respect. In each of these the element of fear is to some degree present – not simply in the sense of being frightened, but as a part of the natural human response to something greater and more powerful than oneself.

Lesson outline 5: infants (Year 1/Year 2)

Theme of activity 'If I were . . .'

Objectives

▶ To give the children practice in developing skills of empathy

▶ To enable the children to enter imaginatively into new and unfamiliar experiences

▶ To provide basic factual information about other people's experiences and life-styles

▶ To contribute to the children's moral development by giving practice in looking ahead to the possible consequences of being in particular situations.

These objectives are fully in line with the aims of RE set out in Chapter 3, and provide the early foundations for the development of an open and sensitive attitude towards unfamiliar religious and cultural practices. In effect, the children are being invited to go as far as they can in putting themselves in other people's shoes.

The lesson could be introduced in a variety of ways. Once again, stories will be of great importance in stimulating the imagination. These can be drawn from both secular and religious sources. Parables could be used to good effect. In the Gospel of Luke there are two which stand out as particularly suitable: in Chapter 10 there is the story of the Good Samaritan, and this could be re-cast to give it a contemporary setting. The children could think about how they would feel if they were in the position of the main characters. In Chapter 15 there is the story of the Prodigal Son, which also lends itself to the same kind of treatment. It is really about two sons, not just one, and the whole narrative reflects a breakdown of relationships because the older son clearly does not understand either his brother or his father. He could not put himself in their positions. Both of these parables could be used to good effect with children of this age, and this is in fact exactly how such stories were often intended to be used. Many (though not all) of the parables of Jesus prompted people to look at something from a different standpoint, and thus learn from the experience.

Obviously, if the children are to be able to imagine themselves in an unfamiliar situation, then at least some aspects of it need to be made familiar to them. Otherwise they have no frame of reference. To be able to picture themselves as blind, or very strong, or very poor, they need some data out of which to construct their imaginary experience. So some facts need to be given. Visitors to the school could be of great help here. A blind person could come into the classroom, perhaps bringing a guide dog, and give the children some idea of what daily routine is like when one cannot see. An elderly person could come and talk about what life was like when he or she was young. Whatever the approach, the children will gain insights into experiences and feelings which are at present beyond them because their own experience has not yet embraced these things. They can 'try them on for size' in their imagination. Responses will not all be the same. In some cases they might find the experience unpalatable, and (like Dorothy in *The Wizard of Oz*) conclude that there's no place like home. In other cases they will be drawn towards the things that they have discovered, and want to repeat the experience or take it further. Both responses are legitimate, and both are evidence of real learning.

Lesson outline 6: infants (Year 1/Year 2)

Theme of activity 'People who help us: the minister/priest'

Objectives

▶ To develop the children's understanding of the concepts of caring and helping, by providing concrete examples

▶ To extend factual knowledge of the work of a religious leader

▶ To give insights into what it means to be religious.

A local minister, of virtually any of the mainstream religious groups, could be invited to spend some time talking with the children and describing what he (or she) does during the course of his or her everyday work. The teacher will need to explain the purpose of the lesson very carefully to the visitor beforehand, because it has been known for visiting ministers to use this opportunity to preach at the children, rather than to teach them.

Children will perhaps already know that ministers (we will use that term for convenience) lead services of worship on special days. They may also know that they perform certain ceremonies such as baptisms, weddings and funerals. But what they probably will not know is that these people also work in other ways – visiting the sick, involving themselves in aspects of community life, attending meetings, studying, possibly teaching in some way, helping people who are in difficulties of many sorts, offering advice and counselling, and generally providing a shoulder to cry on. Far from leading a sheltered life, as many think they do, they are deeply caught up in people's normal joys and sorrows. But why do they do this work?

Behind what the minister does lies the conviction that everyone is important, no matter whether they are rich or poor, young or old, black or white, friends or strangers. This idea can be introduced by using a simple story. In the Gospel of Luke there are several very short parables, more in the nature of analogies, about little things mattering a great deal. These can be found in Luke 15, and they form an introduction to the parable of the Prodigal Son which was mentioned in the previous lesson outline. First there is the story of the man who loses one sheep, and goes to look for it even though he has 99 others. Then there is the illustration of the woman who loses one coin, and works very hard to find it even though she does not really need it. These analogies can be taken at different levels. They can illustrate the idea of something being lost and found again, or (as was probably the original intention) they can be used in this present context to suggest that everyone is of value, no matter how insignificant they may appear to be. It is this idea which underlies the principle of helping: we help because we care, and people help us because they care about us.

The visiting speaker will perhaps make plain to the children that helping can be a costly business. Anyone could do it if it were easy, but it is often very hard. It may mean putting ourselves at risk, or making some sort of sacrifice of time or money or energy. It may mean that we have to go without something so that someone less fortunate can benefit. Helping does not always come naturally!

73

Work of this nature actually serves a variety of purposes. It gives the children some insight into what goes on in a religious community, because that is what the minister represents. If there is eventually to be a visit to a particular place of worship, then the children will have at least a little knowledge of what to expect. Again, it exposes both the ethical and the social dimensions of religion, which we discussed in Chapter 5. It helps the children to understand that religion itself is concerned with real life, and not just with spirituality; they will see that the minister is a normal human being, and not a remote figure who belongs to another dimension. And, of course, it helps to fill out the concept of 'helping' with concrete meaning.

Lesson outline 7: juniors (Year 3/Year 4)

Theme of activity 'Muhammad'

Objectives

▶ To introduce the children to one of the significant figures in a major world religion

▶ To explore the concept of 'greatness'.

This activity is part of a more general theme on some of the major figures in religions of the world. If it is to be effective, the teacher will need to gather information from a reliable source, and again it is stressed that the best are those which come from the religion itself – in this case, Islam. Inevitably, any biography of a major religious figure will be coloured by the enthusiasm of the writer, who, if he or she is a devotee, will always tend to present the best picture possible. However, this is perfectly natural, and need cause no concern. The same thing happens in Christian presentations of the person of Jesus, or Sikh descriptions of Guru Nanak. The esteem in which a religious leader is held by those who follow him is a part of the religion itself.

The work needs to be carefully introduced. It is not just an exercise in biography, but also an exploration of what it is that makes certain people rise above the level of the ordinary, and win the allegiance of thousands of people. It is a study of 'worth', which in fact leads eventually into an exploration of worship or 'worthship', though of course in the case of Muhammad it would be totally wrong to suggest that Muslims worship him as God. They regard him as God's messenger and as the last and greatest Prophet, but they do not see him as divine.

Muhammad was born in 570 CE (AD), and he died in 632 CE. (CE stands for Common Era. It is the equivalent of what Christians refer to as AD.) According to Muslim teaching, he received messages from God (Allah), and repeated them to the people of western Arabia, where he lived. Later on these messages were written down (but not by Muhammad himself), and came to form the Islamic Holy Book (the Qur'an), which ideally is always in the Arabic language. Translations are acceptable, but are not regarded as the true Qur'an.

Muslims believe that there were other prophets before Muhammad, and the list includes people from both the Jewish and Christian religions, such as Moses and Jesus. But Muhammad is regarded as the 'seal' of the prophets – God has nothing more to add to what Muhammad revealed.

Respect is shown to Muhammad by observing the teachings of the Qur'an, by trying to be like him, and by never saying or doing anything that is critical of him. It is wrong for Muslims to make images or pictures of the Prophet, or to portray him in films or plays. Criticism of Muhammad in any form is highly offensive, and according to the Qur'an merits the death penalty.

As the teacher develops this general background of information from reliable sources, so the children will come to see how, in a major religion, respect and reverence are normally shown for a religious leader through

> keeping that person's memory alive
> teaching others about him
> trying to be like him, and holding him up as an example.

An important person is one who exercises some kind of influence. That influence can be exerted in a variety of ways – through leadership, through teaching, through some kind of discovery or invention, or through some major achievement of lasting value. Children could develop the work by identifying other great figures who, in their view, have influenced or are influencing others. Who, in the children's view, deserves to be regarded as important today? Can people still be important long after they are dead, and if so, in what ways? Are television or show business personalities really important, or are they just attractive?

In a different sense, the children could also consider the idea that *everyone* is important, whether they are famous or not. We are all important to those who care about us.

Lesson outline 8: juniors (Year 3/Year 4)

Theme of activity 'The Bible'

Objectives

> ► To introduce the children to the nature of the Christian Bible

> ► To provide factual information about the origins and contents of the Bible

> ► To further the children's understanding of the meaning of the word 'religious'.

This theme is part of a broader topic on 'Books', and the children will need to have access to copies of the Bible in English. It is suggested that the *Good News Bible* is used. Although it is not regarded among scholars as the best translation, it is the clearest in terms of understanding at this particular stage. The teacher will need to point out however, that the line drawings which illustrate this version are not part of the original text! Nor are the short explanatory notes which stand at the head of each of the various books.

The following facts need to be communicated to the children:

> ► The Bible is not really a single volume, but a kind of library. It contains 66 'books' within it: 39 in the first part (the Old Testament) and 27 in the second part (the New Testament).

▶ These books were written a very long time ago, not in Britain but in a different part of the world. So they were not written in the English language. The Old Testament was first written in Hebrew, and the New Testament was first written in a form of everyday Greek. If possible, show the children what these languages look like, and point out that Hebrew is written from right to left. Show on a world map where the country called Palestine was to be found.

▶ Just as in an ordinary library, there are many different kinds of writings in the Bible: history, legends, poetry, laws, and even personal letters. They were collected together so that they could be used in study and in acts of worship. They are community writings which have been preserved because Christians have found them helpful.

▶ The writings in the Bible are now divided up into chapters and verses, with numbers for easy reference, but they were not originally written like that.

▶ Some parts of the Bible are much older than others. They were not all written at the same time, nor were they all written by the same person. In some cases we know the identity of the author, but in others we do not.

It is useful to select some examples from the various writings in the Bible to illustrate the different sorts of literature which it contains. An example of 'law' might be the story of Adam and Eve in the Garden of Eden (Genesis 2:4 to the end of Chapter 3), because that is really about what 'disobedience against God' means. It is *not* a piece of history! A typical legend could be the story of David and Goliath (I Samuel 17). Another version of the same legend can be found in II Samuel 21:19, where the killing of Goliath is attributed to someone else. Looking at the two versions could be used to illustrate how the material in the Bible was assembled from different sources, not always in agreement. Poetry can be found in the book of Psalms, and Psalm 23 could be introduced as a classic example. These instances would be sufficient to give the children an idea of what the Old Testament contains, and the New Testament could be introduced by a brief look at the Gospel of Luke, showing that it is basically all about Jesus.

If the children visit a local church, their attention could be drawn to the conspicuous place which the Bible is given there. It may be lying, either open or closed, on the lectern or reading desk. Sometimes this desk is designed to look like a brass eagle with outstretched wings, symbolising the flight of God's Word (the Bible) across the world.

It is important that the teacher should not try to go too fast at this stage. Before the children can make a close examination of the contents of the Bible they need to gain a clear idea of what sort of book it really is, and of how it was intended to be used within the Christian community. At first they will probably be quite unimpressed, and even bored, by what it says, especially in some of its less absorbing passages. It is also important that the teacher should not pre-empt attitudes to the Bible by calling it 'the Holy Bible' (a term which will be largely unintelligible to the children), or by claiming that Christians think it came to them directly from God (a view which hardly any reputable Christian scholar takes seriously today).

The children could search through the pages of the Bible to find the longest and the shortest books, or they might try to identify which parts are prose and which are poetry (the typesetting usually makes this evident). They could look at some examples of illuminated manuscripts of the Bible, noting how people have tried to write it beautifully as a mark of their respect for its contents. More able children could compare one English version with another (for example, the *Good News Bible* with the *New English Bible*) in order to gain a basic idea of what is involved when a translation has to be made.

It is strongly recommended that the teacher should obtain a copy of a reliable Bible guide book when preparing this class activity. There are several on the market (see Chapter 18). A warning is given against trying to work from memory; experience has shown over and over again that when it comes to remembering accurately what the Bible says, the memory can be very unreliable, and in any case the teacher needs background information to ensure the accuracy of what is presented to the children.

Lesson outline 9: juniors (Year 3/Year 4)

Theme of activity 'Symbols in places of worship'

Objectives

▶ To help the children to recognise what a symbol is, and what it is for

▶ To develop the skill of interpreting religious symbols

▶ To further develop the children's understanding of the nature of religion.

The language of symbolism plays a vital part in all religions, and if the children are to understand what it is and how it works they need to explore it through carefully planned classroom work. The word 'symbol' itself means 'something which stands for something else'. It comes from a Greek term which literally means 'to throw things together', or 'to compare'. In practice, symbolism is a way of communicating an idea by putting it into a special and powerful form. When a symbol is seen or heard, it has to be interpreted. For example, when a team of athletes parades at the opening ceremony of the Olympic Games, the flag of their particular country is carried as a symbol of the nation which they represent. That flag actually *means* something. Or again, a red traffic light symbolises danger and instructs drivers to stop. When a symbol is understood it always has a meaning, but if it is not understood, it becomes something else. The flag becomes merely a piece of cloth, and the red light turns into a lamp.

The aim of this lesson activity is therefore to give the children information about symbols, especially those which might be found inside a place of worship, and to provide opportunities for practice in interpreting them. Ideally, of course, a visit to a place of worship would be the most fruitful way to introduce the work, but if that is not possible, then use could be made of artefacts and pictures in the classroom. Some well known symbols and their meanings are illustrated in Chapter 16, and could be photocopied as teaching material.

The work could be introduced through a discussion of the ways in which symbols play a part in everyday life. A list could be drawn up of those which are most familiar, or a simple visual chart made of trade marks, brand symbols on household goods, logos from national commercial organisations such as the High Street banks, or traffic signs. The task of the children is to identify what each symbol stands for, and to find ways of explaining how the symbols are intended to be used. This could be extended into designing a new symbol to represent a selected idea, perhaps a new school badge or a town crest.

It should be made clear to the children that not all symbols are visual. A sound can have a symbolic meaning (such as a trumpet call), and so also can names. Indeed, a study of the meaning of names can be a rich source of understanding, as can the related idea of naming ceremonies in religious traditions. Symbols do not have to be specially created: ordinary things can be turned into symbols merely by using them in that way. Water is a good example – it is a symbol for life, and is found in many religions. Light is also a common symbol for a variety of ideas. Any or all of these can be used as teaching points, and the teacher will find that the problem is not one of finding enough symbols, but of deciding which to leave out.

Sometimes symbols are used as a kind of secret language, which only 'insiders' are likely to understand. The ancient Christian symbol of the fish, for example, was used to signify the presence of a church fellowship in an area where it was illegal to meet for worship. Secret societies often have their own kinds of symbolism, which mean something to those who are in the know, but nothing to anyone else.

Virtually all religious buildings contain symbols in abundance, and some are actually symbols in their own right. Their shape and overall design frequently have a meaning, and the direction in which they point can be symbolic. So the teacher should bear in mind, when looking for symbols in a place of worship, that some are contained within the very fabric of the place, and not confined to the decorations and the ornaments. A basic plan of a church building will sometimes reveal that it is shaped like a cross (especially if it is very old), or that certain parts of it are on a higher level than others to represent their special importance.

Acts of worship and special ceremonies carried out in a place of worship are also symbolic. We cannot deal with all of them here, but as an example we could highlight the custom of eating and drinking as religious acts. Because people always have to eat and drink to stay alive, these basic activities have been translated into religious symbols. Conversely, fasting (going without food) takes on a special meaning, as well as being a personal discipline. This is clearly seen in the Muslim custom of fasting during daylight throughout the month of Ramadan, and to a lesser degree in the Christian tradition of fasting during Lent. The season of Advent, prior to Christmas, was also originally a time of fasting.

Symbolism in religion spreads into all kinds of activities. Teachers will find that books about ritual, worship, religious art, feasts and festivals and religious dress all draw attention to the symbolic nature of what is done, and it is from such resources that most ideas for practical teaching work can be drawn. Links can also be made with work on language, through a study of symbolic stories.

Lesson outline 10: juniors (Year 5/Year 6)

Theme of activity 'Religious rules'

Objectives

▶ To provide insight into how rules are made and why they are necessary within a community

▶ To demonstrate the nature of religious rules in particular

▶ To show how religious rules are related to religious beliefs

▶ To provide factual information about the rules of religious communities.

This activity should form part of a broader approach to the theme of 'Rules'; what is suggested here is the explicitly religious aspect, but if it is to make much impact it requires that the children shall have a general awareness of the nature and purpose of rules in society as a whole. Through this kind of activity some understanding is gained of how religion contributes to moral education.

It can be introduced by a brief reference to particular words which all have to do with rules in some way:

Laws
Rules
Instructions
Orders
Commandments
Guidelines.

Do all these words mean the same thing? If not, in what ways are they different? Some are stronger than others: laws are meant to be followed, but guidelines are offered only as advice. A short time spent in reflecting upon these words, and trying to determine the distinctions between them, will show the children that this is really a very complex area. Questions will be raised about who has the authority to make laws. How are exceptions to be worked out? What happens when laws are broken? Could we manage without any laws at all? Could a game be played without any rules? What about rules in sport – is it alright to cheat in order to win? What should be done when someone breaks the laws or the rules? How can we ensure that the punishment fits the offence?

Gradually the children will come to appreciate that there are several aspects to laws and rules. There is the fundamental agreement about what is right and what is wrong, and it is on that agreement that all rules are formulated. Then there is the procedure by which the rule comes into force, and the further procedures for ensuring that it is enforced. In addition, there is the complex business of changing the rules, and of knowing when it is right to do so. In the religion of Islam, laws are based upon the teachings of the Qur'an, and because this is the sacred book, believed to have been given by God, those laws cannot be rescinded. In our own Western secular society it is more usual to change laws if it appears that they are no longer desirable or appropriate.

Because religions take the form of communities or organisations, they also have rules. When investigating what these are it is helpful to divide them up into groups, for example:

- ▶ Rules about what the community believes (orthodoxy)
- ▶ Rules about who can be a member of the community (initiation)
- ▶ Rules about authority and leadership (hierarchies)
- ▶ Rules about religious behaviour (ethical codes)
- ▶ Rules about discipline.

If we take Christianity as an example here, we can see that in the first category, rules about belief are often contained in *creeds*. Rules about membership differ somewhat between the various branches of the Christian church, but most follow the rule that someone must be able to give assent to the basic beliefs and promise to follow them, and this is usually done in some kind of *confirmation* ceremony. Rules about authority and leadership are one of the main bones of contention between the different denominations at the present time: in the Roman Catholic Church leadership is vested in the Pope, but in others it may be exercised by a committee or by the members of the local congregation. Many regard the *Bible* as the seat of authority for all Christians. The idea of *priesthood* is closely linked with this. Codes of conduct are generally based upon the principle of *Christian love*, and the life of Jesus is often used as a guideline. Finally, rules about discipline also vary, but in an extreme case many churches would regard *excommunication* as the ultimate sanction; this really means that the offender is not permitted to participate in the sacrament of Holy Communion, and thus would (religiously speaking) 'starve to death'.

What is important is that the children shall see how the rules arise out of the basic principles of the particular religion. In Christianity, the belief that 'God is Love' lays the foundation for Christian life at all levels. In Islam, right and wrong are spelled out by being drawn from the pages of the Qur'an, and the emphasis is upon obedience to God's directives. The very word 'Islam' actually means 'submission to God'.

The essential point to make is that if the rules of a religion are separated from the beliefs upon which they are founded, then they are no longer religious rules at all.

The first part of the Jewish scriptures contains what is known as the Torah (Law), or the Five Books of Moses. These are also in the Christian Old Testament. Children could look at some of the laws contained there, in order to see how they are expressed, and to observe that no clear distinction is made between religious and secular rules; love for God and concern for one's neighbour are seen as essentially the same thing.

Lesson outline 11: juniors (Year 5/Year 6)

Theme of activity 'Ideas about God: God as "Father"'

Objectives

- ▶ To encourage reflection upon the ways in which the word 'God' is used and understood

▶ To present factual information about the teachings of particular religious traditions.

What do people generally mean when they use the word 'God'? Some use it as a swear word. Others use it without having any real idea of what it means. Some use it is a general term for anything that is treated with respect. It is a word which occurs a great deal in religion and religious language, but it does not always carry the same meaning. This activity is aimed at helping the children to find out and reflect upon what people think of when they speak about God, and at the same time to begin to clarify their own thinking in this respect. Although these pupils have now reached the threshold of adolescence, they are still not quite ready to get to grips with abstract theological concepts. But at the same time they are starting to question conventional beliefs and values, and need freedom to put their own ideas to the test.

The teacher will have to exercise caution when undertaking this work. It would be very easy to impose traditional concepts upon the pupils, and almost unconsciously direct them towards images of God which seem more 'right' than others. We all know what happens when those traditional ideas are challenged. A quarter of a century ago, Bishop John Robinson suggested that perhaps the word 'God' ought to be dropped for a while, to allow people to sort out exactly what they mean by it. His point was that the concept has become so confused that what we really need to do is to go back to the beginning and start again.

A start can be made by asking the pupils to write down their own definition of the word 'God', filling it out with descriptive detail. What do they think people mean when this word is used? What might be the characteristics of 'God'? From their responses, a discussion could be developed, searching for areas of similarity and difference. There will be some who give the time-honoured descriptions, and others who offer more individual and original suggestions, pushing their use of metaphor and simile much further. There will also be those who draw a blank, either because they can think of no images at all, or because they regard the concept itself as empty.

Research has shown that during the infant and early junior years, children think of God in very literal terms. He is an old man in the sky, wearing long clothes, and kept busy running the world and answering people's prayers. Gradually this concept begins to change as the children's thinking develops. New words start to be introduced, such as 'power' and 'force', and there is a move away from using only human analogies.

On the basis of this the teacher could demonstrate that in the world's religions there are many different ideas and images of God. Even within a single tradition there can be a rich variety of concepts. Muslims traditionally speak of God having 100 names, only 99 of which are known to mankind. (The hundredth name is sometimes said to be known by camels, which is why they always look so superior!) In the Jewish/Christian culture, the dominant concept of God is that of 'Father', and examples of this can be found in many places in the Bible, for example, Psalm 103:13, Proverbs 3:12, I Corinthians 8:6. In the Gospel of John 5:18 there is a note that Jesus was criticised for speaking of God in this way, as it appeared to make him equal to God, and this is actually the reason why Muslims never use this kind of imagery.

More able pupils could look at the book of Isaiah 40, from verse 12, where there is a poetic account of how that particular writer thought of God; some of the ideas might well match those given by the children themselves.

Why should the word 'Father' be such a popular analogy for God? Because within it the following ideas can be found:

> *Creator of life.* No human birth can take place without a father.
> *Provider.* In earlier times it was always assumed that the father in the family was the breadwinner.
> *Protector.* The father was thought of as the strong figure, defending the weaker members of the family.
> *Guide.* It was the father who made the major decisions, as the head of the family.
> *Loving parent.* The ideal father looks after his family because he loves them, and is even prepared to sacrifice himself for their sakes.

In the modern Western world some of this imagery is regarded as dated and sexist, and the equality of women is being affirmed, with the result that in some quarters the male images of God are being played down, and the concept of God as a mother figure is being brought to the fore. However, this does not alter the Biblical picture, and it can in itself be a fruitful area for discussion with the class.

It is becoming more difficult for the teacher to use the father image as if it represented a commonly accepted ideal within family life. There are many children who come from one-parent families, or from homes in which the father does not conform to the kind of picture presented here. Any discussion about what a father is, or ought to be, can be extremely sensitive, and the teacher will need to know the children's backgrounds very well before taking this too far.

What is important here is that the pupils shall be helped to break free from the habit of picturing God in purely male and human terms (what is technically known as anthropomorphism). They need to appreciate that when we have only human language at our disposal it is inevitable that we will be restricted in the kind of terms that we can use. They should be encouraged to stretch their vocabulary and their imagination, so as to escape from the concrete literalism that is characteristic of younger children, a literalism which, sadly, many adults have never managed to discard.

Lesson outline 12: juniors (Year 5/Year 6)

Theme of activity 'Rituals and ceremonies'

Objectives

> ▶ To explore some of the ways in which religious people express their ideas and beliefs

> ▶ To find out about particular rituals and ceremonies, in terms of what is done and what is meant

> ▶ To encourage attitudes of openness towards people whose religious customs may be different from one's own

> ▶ To help the children to develop skills of interpretation.

Rituals and ceremonies are a central feature of religious practice, and the teacher will need to be very selective in presenting this work. He or she might begin by posing the question 'What is a ritual?' Dictionary definitions can be considered. A ritual, in the narrowest sense, is a form of words, a kind of recitation used in an act of worship. But nowadays the word has been extended to cover the ceremony itself – words and actions together. Very often there is an underlying belief that the effectiveness of what is done is dependent upon the correctness of the ritual: if the wrong words are used, or the actions are somehow at fault, then the performance will not work. But there are also those who regard this as essentially superstitious, and even regard ritual itself as a corruption of true religion.

Yet rituals meet a basic human need. When people come to some point of crisis in their lives they often try to cope with it through ritual. The four major crisis points (birth, coming of age, marriage and death) are full of rituals of many kinds, across virtually all traditions. Even people who would not normally consider themselves religious are drawn to rituals of this sort. All religions have developed their own characteristic ceremonies for such occasions. The children could explore birth rituals, such as the Islamic custom of speaking words from the Qur'an into a newborn child's ear, or the Jewish custom of giving the firstborn son to God and then buying him back ('redeeming' him). Another approach would be to look at initiation rites, such as a Jewish Bar-mitzvah ceremony for a 13-year-old boy, or a Christian confirmation rite. It is not unknown for a teacher to invite a local (co-operative) minister or priest to conduct a simulation of a wedding ceremony in the classroom, explaining what the different elements of it actually mean. This would include not only the form of the ceremony, but also the background to the clothes which are traditionally worn, and the religious principles behind the concept of marriage.

The range of possibilities here is vast, and there are now many excellent books and other resources available to help the teacher who is unsure of the details (see Chapter 18). No single lesson activity could possibly exhaust the potential. Even an exploration of rituals associated with death should not be dismissed as unsuitable: there is a great deal to be said in favour of taking this as a classroom theme, and looking at it objectively, perhaps starting with a study of the 'In memoriam' columns in the newspaper, or a visit to the local cemetery, to find out how people express their feelings. Ancient burial customs expose beliefs about what comes after death, and this could raise interesting and important points for classroom consideration.

CHAPTER 12

VISITING A PLACE OF WORSHIP

On several occasions throughout the earlier part of this book mention has been made of the value of visiting a place of worship. It has long been a curious irony in primary school education that visits to such places have not yielded very much by way of substantial RE. This seems to be largely because many teachers tend to lay all or most of their emphasis upon the historical aspect, treating the visit as if it were to a religious museum. As a result, opportunities are commonly missed to develop in the children any real awareness of the actual nature of the building. Furthermore, the visits generally take place when the building is not in use, so the children come away with the impression that they have been looking at some kind of relic, important perhaps in the past, but now virtually obsolete. This is particularly true when the visit is to an old building, because the sense of antiquity is even more strongly reinforced.

This chapter offers advice on how a visit to a place of worship might be arranged so as to be more productive of good RE. We shall focus in particular upon a visit to a Christian church, but note will also be taken of what is involved in visiting centres in other religious traditions.

The objectives must be clear

The teacher's first task is to identify the purpose of the visit, and what it is in particular that he or she wishes the children to learn from it. It is not sufficient merely to go and look around. A place of worship could, of course, provide valuable learning in the spheres of environmental studies, or art, or (as we have noted) history, and this is perfectly valid: but here we are concerned specifically with RE, and it is this aspect of the curriculum which needs to be uppermost in the teacher's mind. The questions to be asked, and answered, are basically these:

▶ What exactly is a church?

▶ What is the building for?

▶ What happens inside it, and why?

▶ Why was it built just here?

▶ What sort of people use it?

▶ What does it contain?

The answer to the first question is that the word 'church' has three distinct meanings. It can refer to the actual building (which is the sense in which we are thinking of it now). It can also refer to the people who use it (as when we speak of 'joining the church'). And it can describe the whole worldwide institution of Christianity, throughout history (as when we talk about 'the spread of the church'). It is important that the children gain some awareness of these different uses of the word, because otherwise there could be confusion in their minds. The answers to the other questions are likely to be found by actually exploring the building and making enquiries of the people who belong to it.

Practical considerations

Which church?

Which is the best church building to visit? Obviously, the one which offers the greatest number of learning opportunities, and is conveniently reached in the time available. The impulse to head without question for the local parish church should be resisted, because it may not be the best choice. There may be another, possibly of a different denomination, which has more potential. The belief that the parish church is the 'real' one, and that all the others are of a lower status, stubbornly lingers on, but cannot be sustained in this present day and age. A preliminary survey to check the possibilities will pay ample dividends.

Making the first contact

Initial contact will need to be made with the minister or priest in charge, to fix a convenient date and to outline the educational purpose of the visit. Churches are not public places, always available to anyone who wishes to drop in; they are private property, and the teacher who simply turns up on the doorstep with a group of children could find that the building is either closed or is otherwise engaged. This may appear to be a statement of the obvious, but it is by no means unknown for situations of this kind to occur.

The teacher must retain control

Although the visit is to a place of worship, it is still a part of the children's school-led education, and for this reason it must remain the teacher's responsibility. One of the most common problems encountered on visits to churches is that the minister or priest will effectively take over, making all the decisions about what the children are to see and do. Some places of worship are visited so often that the authorities there have established a fixed pattern of guided tours, and these may be quite unsuitable for the intended purpose. It is therefore of crucial importance that the teacher should remain in control of what happens, within the bounds of courtesy to the hosts. Some ministers, too, are not altogether aware of the skills required in dealing with young children, and can pitch the level too high or too low. Others mistakenly think that this is an opportunity to preach at the children. Every effort should be made to avoid subjecting the class to a lengthy and over-zealous talk, and much can be done by a careful preliminary discussion to plan exactly what is to take place.

Choosing adult helpers

Naturally the normal rules will apply concerning the ratio of adults to children for supervision purposes; but when arranging for extra helpers it is a good idea to seek out any who might themselves be members of the church. Their presence can then be doubly valuable, because as well as supervising the children they can act as resources for information. If this point is made to the minister during the preliminary discussion, he or she will often be able to identify people to fill this role.

Notifying parents

A note will need to be sent to the parents of the children concerned, telling them of the intention to visit the church. It is particularly important that this is done, because they have the legal right to opt their children out if they wish to do so. It is always possible that some parents will object to their children going inside a church of a particular denomination, even though the same children participate normally in classroom RE. Only a very small minority are likely to react in this way, but nevertheless the opportunity has to be given to them. If the visit is to a mosque or a synagogue, or indeed to a place of worship of any non-Christian religion, then the likelihood of this happening is somewhat increased. Sometimes the fears and prejudices of parents who are anxious about such a visit can be allayed by a careful explanation of its purpose.

Available facilities

The teacher should not overlook the importance of checking on the facilities available to the visiting party. Where are the toilets? Is there a suitable place where the children could eat a packed lunch? Could a room be set aside as work space for the children to consult books, write notes, draw pictures or complete worksheets? Does the church have its own guide book to which the children could refer, and is it in language which they can understand? Are there any parts of the building to which the children are not allowed access, for reasons of safety or because the place is sacred? Are the children expected to dress in a particular way, and are there any items of special clothing available for lending to those who have forgotten about this (such as head coverings)? Points of this nature, though small in themselves, are important and should be clarified prior to the visit if everything is to run smoothly.

Hidden treasures

Not everything that the church possesses will be out on open display. Certain items, especially those which are intrinsically valuable, are likely to be locked away for safe keeping. These would include special records and documents, such as the baptismal register or the chalice used at the service of Holy Communion or the Mass. If asked to do so, the priest or minister will probably bring these out for the children to see and even handle under supervision. He, too, is also a 'resource' by virtue of the fact that he is a part of the church institution, so the children could look at him, perhaps when he is wearing his vestments, and find out about his work, and what his special clothes mean.

The importance of the outside of the building

Unlike some buildings, the outside of a church can be just as interesting and informative as the inside. If possible, therefore, the visit should be planned to take place when the weather is likely to be fine, so that the children have an opportunity to explore the exterior. If there is a graveyard, or a lych gate, or gargoyles, or interesting foundation stones, these in themselves can provide material for follow-up work back in school. Even the shape of the building, often seen more clearly from the outside than from within, can be meaningful.

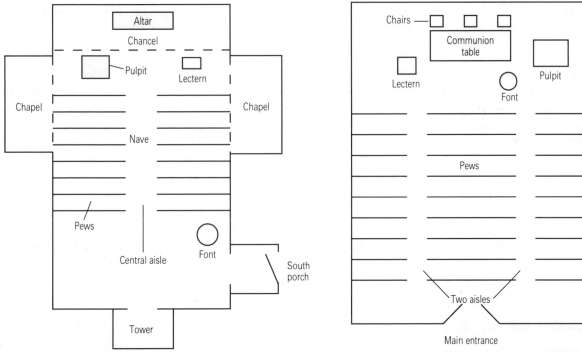

Figure 12.1 Plan of a typical Anglican church   Figure 12.2 Plan of a typical Free church

Inside the building

Inside, the children can explore the general layout, the position and purpose of the fixtures and fittings, the craftsmanship, the stained glass windows (if there are any), the memorials, and anything else that they see or is drawn to their attention. The aim should be to find out why it is like that, and what everything is for. How are the altar (or the communion table in a Free church), the lectern, the font and the pulpit used? Who uses them, and when? Is there any symbolism present, and what does it mean?

There will probably be hymn books and prayer books somewhere in the church. These will provide clues to the teachings and beliefs of that particular kind of church, and they will also throw light upon what happens during a service of worship. If it can be arranged, a few copies of these might be borrowed on a short-term basis by the teacher, so that closer study of them can be made back in the classroom. Opportunities to do this are commonly missed, yet they can be extremely useful for developing the children's understanding.

Somewhere inside the church there may be posters and notices which advertise special church activities and meetings. These are important, too. They are evidence of the things in which the church is involved, through its organisations. The children could look at these, and gain an idea of what the ongoing life of the church community is like.

The experiential aspect

Children will often respond to the 'feel' of a church building. They will describe it as 'holy' or 'frightening' or 'weird'. This is something which the teacher can take up with them when the visit is over. Can they explain why it felt like that? Did the buildings have a special kind of atmosphere, and what words would be most suitable to express the feelings it evoked?

If the minister is accustomed to working with young children, he might be persuaded to arrange a simulation of a particular ceremony so that they can actually experience it for themselves. Some, for example, have agreed to 'baptise' a doll brought in by the children, for which a name has been chosen during classroom work on names. Much will depend upon local circumstances and relationships, but it is worth finding out if this is possible, so as to give the children a very special kind of learning experience. Others have demonstrated the basics of a service of Holy Communion, allowing the children to look closely at the bread and wine, and in some cases even to taste them to see what they are like. Although in some situations this would be considered improper, other ministers would understand that this is how children learn, and would not object to doing this. The same general principle applies to experiencing the *sound* of the church organ. If the organist can be present, the children can hear what the organ sounds like, and even sing a familiar hymn to organ accompaniment. This is far more meaningful than merely looking at the organ pipes.

Follow-up work

Normally an educational visit is followed up afterwards in the classroom, when the children have an opportunity to focus in a more settled way upon particular aspects of what was seen and done. Apart from the obvious task of writing 'Thank you' letters to the priest or minister, they could (as we have suggested) spend time looking at some of the hymns and prayers normally used by the congregation. It is quite remarkable how rarely such an opportunity is given, even in relation to the hymns and prayers that are used in the school's act of collective worship. Another possibility is to arrange a further visit to a different kind of place of worship, so that comparisons can be made. The value of this will depend upon the age of the children: older ones will gain more than the younger ones. Drawings of certain features of the church could be made, possibly based on rough sketches or photographs obtained during the actual visit. These should be supplemented by explanatory notes, so that there is some reinforcement of the children's understanding.

Older pupils could work in groups to design a place of worship which, in their view, would meet the needs of a contemporary Christian congregation.

If the church which was visited is fairly old, then it was probably once the centre of the life of that community. More able children could research into this, to find out how the church contributed to the social structures, and to identify what sort of a legacy it has left behind.

Visiting a non-Christian place of worship

Although the children can gain a good deal from visiting a non-Christian place of worship, there are certain practicalities which need to be considered, and which can make such a visit rather less straightforward than going to a church. First of all, the children will probably be unable to read the notices and the books, because these will be in an unfamiliar language. Second, the leader of the community may not be entirely fluent in English, and consequently will be harder to understand. Third, members of ethnic minority communities are not always very familiar with the British way of learning through experience and discovery, and they could therefore be ill at ease when large numbers of children are turned loose on their premises. Fourth, some of the cultural aspects of the religion probably need to be explored before the visit can reap its full rewards. Consequently, experience suggests that a visit to a non-Christian centre is best made when the children are a little older; it is doubtful whether infants can gain a great deal of benefit. However, there are exceptions to this. If the school is located in an area where a high proportion of the children actually come from the minority groups, then the place of worship would for them be their natural starting point, and they would already be familiar with the cultural background and the language. In their case it might well be the visit to the church which needs to be deferred!

Teachers' background knowledge

Teachers who are not regular churchgoers may understandably feel that their own lack of background knowledge about a place of worship will cause problems. This need not be a serious difficulty. There are now many good books on the market which will guide the uninitiated through the complexities of distinguishing between the numerous Christian denominations, and a rough and ready sketch is provided in Chapter 15. The list of resources in Chapter 18 identifies more detailed sources of information.

CHAPTER 13

MEASURING SUCCESS IN RELIGIOUS EDUCATION

When RE first became part of the state school curriculum it inherited the aims and objectives of the church school, and these were directed largely towards encouraging pupils to adopt the Christian way of life. Success was thus measured in terms of the extent to which children conformed to the moral and doctrinal standards of the church. Today, however, the aims are very different (see Chapter 3), and with those changing aims there has come a need to think again about appropriate methods of testing whether they have been achieved.

There are always three aspects to be considered in assessment and evaluation. These are:

1 *The content of the teaching*
Was the content worthwhile? Was it accurate, objective, fair and balanced? Most teachers will admit that on occasions they have given children work which was really a waste of time and effort, either because it was intended to do no more than keep them occupied, or because it was inherently unproductive of serious learning. The process of assessment must always include the discipline of evaluating actual lesson content.

2 *The method of presentation*
Was the work introduced in the most effective way, or could it have been done differently? Was it stimulating? Was it imaginative? Was it accurately matched to the children's age and ability levels? Was the organisation efficient? Was enough time allowed for a proper coverage of the chosen area, or was it superficial? Did it go on too long? If teaching aids such as books, pictures and artefacts were used, were they employed to full advantage, and were they in themselves accurate and up-to-date?

3 *The children's learning*
The third aspect is that of the children's learning, and this of course is what matters most. The quality of the lesson content and of the way in which it was taught will obviously affect the levels of achievement, as also will the children's inherent ability and the general environment in which they are working.

All attempts to measure success in teaching must take the above three factors into account. So, with these in mind, how can progress and achievement in RE be measured? If the criteria are no longer what they used to be, what are they now? The first step towards finding an answer to this is to refer back to the basic aims of RE which were set out in Chapter 3, because all assessment and evaluation has to be rooted in a clear understanding of the purpose behind the learning. If a man does not know where he is going, then he has no way of telling whether or not he has arrived.

If these stated aims are turned now into questions, they can become both a checklist for the process of assessment and a basis for the formulating of measuring techniques. Naturally some of the aims, because they are long-term, will not be achieved at all in the primary school, and others will be only partially realised. We have already observed that the particular role of the primary school is to lay the foundations, rather than to complete the building. Nevertheless, by using the general aims as a starting point, key assessment questions can be framed, as set out below:

Assessment checklist

1 Are the children beginning to understand what the word 'religion' means?
2 Are they beginning to acquire the language skills and vocabulary which are needed to explore religious phenomena?
3 Are they becoming better informed about some of the basic facts relating to religion and religious behaviour?
4 Is there evidence that they are increasing in sensitivity towards religious beliefs and customs, and that they are becoming more open to new ideas?
5 Are they becoming more aware of the basic features of the Christian religion, and of the ways in which it has influenced their culture and environment?
6 Do they appreciate that particular experiences in life (such as birth, coming of age, marriage and death) seem to raise the most important religious questions?
7 Are the children becoming more able to make links between religious ideas and other areas of experience? Can they see relevant and genuine connections?
8 Is there any evidence that they are maintaining their curiosity about religion and about those things with which religion is fundamentally concerned? Are they asking religious questions?
9 Are they seeing any connection between religion and issues of right and wrong?

All teachers know that a great deal of their overall assessment of the children is based upon general experience of them within the day-to-day classroom situation, and in the playground. What counts most is knowledge of the child as a person, and judgements tend to be made on the basis of constant observation of behaviour patterns and attitudes, as well as of standards reached and maintained across the curriculum. But to this there have to be added more precise and objective procedures for measuring actual levels of achievement. Methods of testing need to be worked out, which are capable of producing valid results that are less prone to be affected by the teacher's personal opinions.

Attainment targets

For all of those subjects which fall within the National Curriculum, clear attainment targets have been or are being established. In the case of RE, however, it is open to Local Education Authorities to set their own such targets if they wish to do so, and some have already set this process in motion.

Whatever one may think of particular targets, in terms of their realism or desirability, it cannot be denied that a fixed goal does provide the best kind of basis for measuring the achievement of individual children. Naturally there is room for argument, especially about those children who are in some way exceptional, but it is reasonable to assume that the process of measuring attainment does demand some kind of milestone placed along the child's path of learning. When set out in the form of age-related targets, they might for example appear as follows:

Attainment targets for Reception infants

By the end of the first year in the infant school, children should be able to:

- ▶ demonstrate the ability to co-operate with other children, and to share equipment, resources and ideas

- ▶ show clear signs of feeling generally secure in the classroom environment, and of being ready to explore new ideas and experiences

- ▶ recognise and know something about particular special occasions such as birthdays, holidays, and some major religious festivals such as Christmas and Easter

- ▶ demonstrate a growing appreciation of the ways in which their five senses can be used

- ▶ show an awareness of what a family is, and of what it means to belong to a family

- ▶ Recognise and understand the meaning of some basic religious terms, (for example, 'prayers', 'church')

- ▶ display a degree of self-awareness.

Attainment targets for Year 1

By the end of the second year in the infant school, children should be able to:

- ▶ work with others as members of a group

- ask questions in a confident way, and show some degree of independence in searching out answers

- share and talk about personal feelings and experiences, and listen to what others have to say about their own

- express ideas in a variety of ways (for example, drawing, painting, acting, writing simple words)

- recognise obvious religious phenomena (for example, a church building, a wedding ceremony, a religious festival).

Attainment targets for Year 2

By the end of the third year in the infant school, children should be able to:

- work with others in a way which shows consideration for other people's feelings and needs

- reflect upon the things that have happened to them, and recognise important experiences

- project themselves into imaginary situations and think about what it would be like to be in other people's shoes

- understand at a simple level what is involved in caring, sharing and helping

- express their ideas and feelings in a greater variety of ways and with more precision

- recall and recount some of the major features of the festivals of Christmas and Easter

- talk about simple issues of right and wrong.

Attainment targets for Year 3

By the end of the first year in the junior school, children should be able to:

- understand, at a simple level, the concept of 'importance', and be able to identify someone who is important in the sphere of religion

- show a general awareness of the life of Jesus (and/or another significant religious leader)

- ▶ appreciate that there are many different religions in the world beside Christianity, and that there are different kinds of churches
- ▶ recognise the Bible, and understand that it has a special significance within the Christian religion
- ▶ describe in general terms what a symbol is and how it is used
- ▶ identify some of the things that go on inside a place of worship.

Attainment targets for Year 4

By the end of the second year in the junior school, children should be able to:

- ▶ show a general familiarity with the structure and history of the Bible, and know that it is a collection of literature
- ▶ recognise and interpret some familiar religious symbols
- ▶ describe the main features of a church, and identify the central items inside it
- ▶ know something about the teachings of Jesus and of another major religious personality
- ▶ identify an increased range of religious signs and symbols, in both Christianity and other religions
- ▶ show some understanding of how religion affects people's lives and behaviour.

Attainment targets for Year 5

By the end of the third year in the junior school, children should be able to:

- ▶ recognise and discuss ways in which religion has affected their culture and environment
- ▶ demonstrate an understanding of the nature and necessity of rules and laws, and appreciate the part they play in religion
- ▶ handle the Bible in terms of identifying its main parts, and knowing something of its chronological framework
- ▶ show readiness to listen to other beliefs, and to treat them with respect and seriousness even when not agreeing with them

> ▶ identify and describe some of the features of major religious festivals and special days, in both Christianity and another religion
>
> ▶ appreciate that religion is concerned with meaning and purpose.

Attainment targets for Year 6

By the end of the fourth year in the junior school, children should be able to:

▶ recognise the major dimensions of religion (see Chapter 5)

▶ describe in general terms the main teachings of Jesus

▶ demonstrate a reasonable degree of knowledge about the religious history of their own immediate locality

▶ discuss in a general way what is meant by the word 'God'

▶ name some of the other major religions found in Britain today

▶ understand something of the importance of ritual in everyday life and more specifically in religion

▶ recognise that religion plays a very important part in many people's lives, and identify examples of religious vocations.

The attainment targets described above are, of course, very general in nature, and there will be many children who exceed or fall short of them. They should be seen as no more than examples of what might reasonably be expected of primary school pupils at particular points in their schooling, based upon the overall aims of RE within the curriculum. As we have already noted, Local Education Authorities are at liberty to establish their own targets, and they may well formulate them quite differently from those set out here.

Methods of testing

Methods of testing will obviously vary according to the nature of the particular target. As a general guide, one could divide the tests into three distinct areas: factual knowledge, understanding and sensitivity.

Factual knowledge

Factual knowledge (of which there has to be some for any adequate understanding of religion!) can be assessed through straightforward questioning of an unambiguous kind:

'In which country was Jesus born?'
'Who was the founder of the Sikh religion?'
'What do Muslims do during the month of Ramadan?'
'Which foods are Jewish people not permitted to eat?'

The children's answers to such questions as these will be either correct or incorrect, and it is a simple matter to produce a score which reflects the accuracy of their knowledge. This then would become an element within their record of achievement.

Understanding

To test children's understanding as distinct from factual knowledge, questions need to be framed rather differently:

'Why was Jesus put to death?'
'Explain the meaning of a baptismal ceremony.'
'What do you think might make someone wish to become a monk?'
'Why do some people prefer a church wedding to one which takes place in a registry office?'
'What point was Jesus making when he told the story of the Good Samaritan?'

These questions require the children to interpret the facts, rather than merely to repeat them. The teacher's task in assessing the answers is to make a judgement about the quality (and to some extent also the accuracy) of that interpretation.

Sensitivity

The degree to which children are sensitive to religious ideas, or to which they display attitudes of openness towards different beliefs and customs, is more difficult to assess objectively. One way of doing it is to give them a controversial issue (for example, arranged marriages), and ask them to divide a sheet of paper down the middle, writing 'arguments for' on one side and 'arguments against' on the other. Those who can see points on both sides could be considered more sensitive than those who see only one point of view. But much of the assessment in this area is likely to be based upon a more general observation of the child's readiness to listen to other points of view and to treat them with respect. To some extent, sensitivity will also be revealed in the sphere of their *understanding* discussed above.

Records of achievement

Records of achievement are very much a personal matter, and they can vary in their format not only from school to school but even from one class to another. In some cases there are fixed lay-outs required by the LEA, to facilitate the passing on of information between the different stages of the children's schooling. Whatever form these records take, they will generally include two kinds of information. There will be a record of the work covered (that is, a summary of the topics or areas of work in which the children have been engaged throughout the period under review), and there will also be an indication of the standards reached by each child, supplemented by more general comments about attitude, ability, comparison with earlier performance, etc.

The actual style of the record may well be influenced by the question of whether it is to be confidential within the school, or whether it is to be open to inspection by parents or other interested parties. It is now normal for records to be accessible to parents, so that a greater formality of presentation is usually adopted, but this is still linked to the 'human touch' added through direct conversation. It is plain that the record must be such that it gives more than a generalised picture, and a possible format might look something like the example in Figure 13.1.

Figure 13.1 Example record sheet

Name of child: . . . .

Date of birth: . . . .   School: . . . .

Class: . . . .   Class teacher: . . . .

Work covered in RELIGIOUS EDUCATION during the period from . . . .   to . . . .

Topic(s)/Themes/Areas:

. . . .

. . . .

. . . .

. . . .

. . . .

Record of achievement:

1   Factual knowledge: test/examination score: . . . .

2   Level of understanding: [graded A to D]: . . . .

3   Attitude [teacher's appraisal]:

. . . .

. . . .

. . . .

D

INFORMATION AND RESOURCES

In this section you will find five sub-sections of useful information, to which reference can be made during the preparation of classroom work:

▶ a brief sketch of some of the world's major religions

▶ an outline of the main branches of British Christianity

▶ a selection of Christian symbols and their meanings

▶ addresses where further information and resources can be obtained

▶ a list of books which will be found valuable for both the teacher and the children.

CHAPTER
14

THE WORLD'S MAJOR RELIGIONS:
A THUMBNAIL SKETCH

It has been said that there are as many different religions in the world as there are people, and to some extent there is truth in that statement. But for practical purposes we can identify the major religions of mankind as:

> Christianity
> Islam
> Judaism
> Hinduism
> Buddhism
> Sikhism.

The above list is not in any order of priority, and judgements about what qualifies as a major religion are bound to be somewhat subjective. The list is made up of those faiths which primary school children are most likely to hear about or encounter directly, and readers should not assume that other religions, not included here, are deemed to be unimportant. We will describe each, in the order given.

Christianity

Christianity is the religion which has most deeply influenced British life and culture, and it is the one which the Education Reform Act of 1988 has singled out for that reason. Yet it is not actually native to this country. It has its roots in the Middle East, in the Jewish religion, almost 2000 years ago. At that time the Roman Empire dominated most of the civilised world, and the Jews were eagerly looking for their promised Messiah ('Chosen One') who would lead them back to freedom. There were numerous claimants to this title, but one, Jesus of Nazareth, aroused special interest. His activities as a travelling preacher, healer and teacher brought him both fame and notoriety, and eventually he was put to death by crucifixion while still a young man.

After his death, some of his former followers claimed that he had risen from the grave, and that he had shown himself to them in mysterious circumstances. This led them to conclude that he really was the one they had been waiting for, and they began to speak of him in terms suggesting that he was divine. Their certainty of his living presence led them to spread their beliefs, both by word of mouth and through writing. Some of what they wrote has come down to us, in the form of copies passed from generation to generation, and from one Christian community to another. The best known of these writings are those which eventually found a place within the Christian scriptures, namely, the four Gospels and the letters of Paul of Tarsus, the first major Christian missionary.

Because the first Christians were Jewish (as was Jesus himself), it was natural that the Jewish Bible would continue to be respected as a sacred book; so, together with the later Gospels and letters, it was preserved as the Christian Bible. By the middle of the fourth century after Jesus it had reached its final stage of development, and became fixed in the form with which we are now familiar.

Gradually Christianity and Judaism grew apart. As a result of missionary activity, Christianity spread across the Roman world, despite strong opposition and persecution. When the Roman Emperor Constantine himself became a Christian, it was legalised and became the official religion of the Empire. Its centre of gravity shifted from Jerusalem to Rome, laying the foundations for what eventually became known as Roman Catholicism.

The history of Christianity is one of mixed fortunes. There have been serious divisions within its ranks – first the 'Great Schism' which split it into East and West, and then later the Reformation within the Western branch, which was both a rebellion against the authority of the Roman church and an affirmation that the Bible is the only true basis for Christian belief and life. There have also been times when Christians did things which they later came to regret, especially when there was more than a hint of political opportunism behind the supposed spirituality. But it is also true that out of the Christian tradition there have come many valuable insights and important contributions to human well-being. Social reforms were often initiated by men and women who saw the relevance of their Christian principles to the conditions of their times.

At the heart of Christianity lies the conviction that there is one God, from whom everything takes its origin, and who has made himself known most fully in the person of Jesus of Nazareth. All branches of the church agree on this, and teach that Christians have access to the power of God through the things that Jesus did. It is a basic Christian belief that the new life which Jesus is said to have made possible through his resurrection is now available to all who attach themselves to him through faith. There are differences of emphasis, as we shall see later in our survey of the main Christian denominations (Chapter 15), and sometimes these are of major importance. But the different churches still hold sufficient in common for us to be able to say that they share the same basic religious position.

Islam

Islam is, in terms of history, a more recent religion than Christianity. Its beginnings can be traced back to Muhammad, who was born in the city of Mecca in western Arabia in 570 CE and died in 632 CE. Muhammad believed that he had been singled out by God to deliver a moral and religious directive to mankind, affirming belief in only one God and demanding high standards of personal and social behaviour. The keynote of the message was that of submission to God's will, and this is what the name of the religion (Islam) actually means.

The divine directives were eventually set down in writing, and form the Holy Book of Islam, the Qur'an. Its words are accepted by Muslims as coming directly from God, and are never regarded as the ideas of Muhammad himself, who was simply God's messenger. It is a basic principle in Islam that the Qur'an should be studied in its original language of Arabic, since that is the language God chose to use. A translation, though useful, is not given the same high status. The Prophet himself is always highly revered, and his personal example is seen as guidance for living. A complete month in the Islamic calendar is set aside to honour his birth and life.

Muslims teach that mankind is by nature incapable of knowing ultimate truth, and must therefore rely upon what God has revealed. Muhammad is the last and the greatest of all the prophets, so there can be no alteration or amendment to the words that he revealed. The task of an Islamic government is therefore not to make laws, but to ensure that the laws of the Qur'an are properly observed.

All Muslims are taught that there are certain things which they must do as obligations, and certain other things which they are not permitted to do. It is the continuing responsibility of Islamic lawyers to explain what these are. There are five obligations which form the basic structure for a Muslim's life: consciously affirming the simple creed, praying (five times a day), giving to charity, fasting during the ninth month of the year, and making a once-in-a-lifetime pilgrimage to the Holy City of Mecca.

Like Christianity, Islam is a missionary religion, and has spread outwards from its Arabian birthplace, though it has retained the Arabic language as its sacred tongue. Today its centre of gravity is the Indian sub-continent. Islam, too, has distinguishable groups within it, the main ones being the Sunnis ('orthodox') and the Shi'ites ('partisans'). The roots of this distinction go back to the early years of Islam, when there was a dispute about who was qualified to succeed the Prophet Muhammad.

Today Islam ranks as perhaps the second largest religion in the world, next to Christianity, though some hold that Hinduism has more followers. Whatever may be the precise truth, there are certainly more Muslims in Britain than there are followers of any other non-Christian faith. There are several Islamic cultural centres established here, from which information can readily be obtained (see Chapter 17), and mosques (prayer houses) are being built in many parts of the country.

Judaism

The Jewish religion has been in Britain for a very long time, but political persecution brought many more Jewish people here during the first half of the present century. It is a basic principle among Orthodox Jews that, while acknowledging and respecting the fact that they are dispersed in many countries, Israel is their true homeland. They teach that God chose them from among all the nations of the earth to be his special people, and they strive to retain their special identity. God has made a 'covenant' with them, and in order to remain within it they must adhere to the God-given law (Torah) which sets out what is required of them.

In order to ensure that they do not become absorbed into their host cultures, and thereby lose their identity as Jews, they have preserved their Hebrew language, and many of them still insist that it is wrong to inter-marry with Gentiles. Their past history is remembered and taught to successive generations through special festivals and holy days. History is particularly important to Jews because they see it as the stage on which God is working out his divine purposes for mankind. He is best understood through the things that he has done.

Judaism is not a missionary religion, like Christianity and Islam. As far as Jews are concerned, God has already chosen those whom he wants, and consequently it is not easy to enter Judaism if someone is not Jewish by birth. Some have become Jews through marriage, but the process of acceptance is quite difficult.

It has been argued, with some justification, that Judaism is not so much a religion as a way of life. Certainly the basic beliefs are quite simple, and, more significantly, it is a faith which is based more upon the home than upon the place of worship. The Jewish Temple in Jerusalem was destroyed in the year 70 CE (AD), and has never been rebuilt because of political circumstances. Today there is a magnificent Muslim mosque standing upon the site. Synagogues have now come into their own as places where Jews can meet, study and pray. But synagogues are not temples as such, and there is no active priesthood. Teachers, known as rabbis, give instruction, guidance and discipline. Orthodox Jews are still looking forward to the day when their temple in Jerusalem will be restored, so that the old ways can flourish once more.

There is a modern movement within Judaism known as Reform Judaism, in which some of the older traditions have been either modified or dropped altogether. Men and women are permitted to pray together in the synagogue, and there are even women rabbis, something which would never be tolerated in Orthodox Judaism. Reform Judaism is strong in the USA, and now has its own central organisation and its own colleges for training its leaders.

Hinduism

Hinduism is a highly complex religious tradition, more in the nature of a collection of religions than a single identifiable entity. As its name suggests, it is closely linked with India, but there are Hindus from other races. The range of beliefs and practices is extraordinarily wide, so much so that it is really very hard to pick out anything that might be considered essential. It had no founder, and there is no creed or official set of teachings. The most important thing in Hinduism is not really belief at all, but behaviour. God is thought of as being everywhere at all times, without limits and formless. The word used for God is 'Brahman', which is neither a male nor a female term. Some Hindus, though not all, think that the human soul is a spark from God, but others deny this and see it as independent. All generally agree that the soul had no birth and will never die; it continues in ever-changing forms, through a process sometimes known as reincarnation or, more correctly, transmigration. In every new form of life, the rewards or penalties earned in the previous existence are evident.

Because of the belief that all life is sacred, Hindus are generally opposed to killing any living thing. Most are vegetarian, at least to a limited degree, and some are totally against eating anything that is obtained by hurting or killing a living creature. The 'sacred cow' of Hinduism is a good example of this reverence for animals.

Some Hindu teachings appear to Western eyes as very superstitious. Astrology features powerfully in Hindu customs, especially in marriage but also in business affairs. The custom of reading palms to tell fortunes has its origins here.

There are many thousands of temples and places of worship in Hinduism, and the number of scriptures is so vast that even today new ones are being found, and not all of the others have yet been published.

Hindus speak of having three debts to pay during their lifetime. They have a debt to their parents, and this means that parents and ancestors are greatly honoured. Second, they have a debt to the wise teachers of the past, and this means that they themselves must also pursue wisdom. Third, they have a debt to pay to God, and this is why they worship and treat God's creation in a respectful way.

Worship involves many complex rituals, some of which are extremely ancient and have largely lost their original significance. Hospitality must be offered to anyone, and especially to travelling holy men. Charity must be given to the poor, whoever they are. There are several important festivals, prominent among which are the New Year (somewhere between March and April), and Diwali (Festival of Lights). The festival of Holi in the spring is a much-loved occasion, when old quarrels are forgotten and everyone tries to visit friends.

Hindus are taught that worldly possessions are purely transitory, and that what matter most are the things of the spirit. As a consequence of this teaching, many become wandering monks, who give up almost everything and travel from place to place with begging bowls. Some take up residence in temples and make a living by performing special religious services for the local population.

Buddhism

Like Hinduism, Buddhism also exists in different forms. Early Buddhism, known as Theravada, is not strictly speaking a religion at all, but a philosophy. Later Buddhism, however, has developed customs and beliefs which bear the marks of genuine religion. It can be traced back to the sixth century BCE (Before the Christian Era, i.e. BC), in the teachings of a man called Siddhartha Gautama, from north-east India. Because of his theories he became known as 'the Enlightened One' or 'the Buddha'. He was trying to discover why everything changes and decays, and he concluded that the cause lies in *craving*. All change, suffering and restlessness are due to the desire to hold on to what is really transitory; so he taught what was essentially a programme of self-discipline.

The programme which the Buddha taught consisted of three main elements: morality, meditation and wisdom. All three are intended to be pursued together, not one after the other, but the moral element stands supreme, because without it the others would not be taken seriously. It involves sexual purity, honesty, and abstaining from taking life and from taking any form of drugs. Meditation requires what is known as 'right thinking', and involves disciplining the mind so as to concentrate only upon worthy things. Buddhist wisdom involves becoming aware of the things that the Buddha himself discovered – that everything is impermanent, and that nothing ever

103

remains the same. Attachment to what is really fleeting is the root of all suffering. It is only when we accept this that life becomes bearable.

As Buddhism developed, it relaxed its grip upon Indian culture, but found fertile soil in the Oriental world. China showed great interest in it, as also did Japan and Tibet. Each of these cultures added its own special flavour to the Buddhist philosophy, and as a result different forms of Buddhism emerged. Ceylon (Sri Lanka) adopted it with enthusiasm, and is now the country with the longest unbroken Buddhist tradition. It is also where we can witness the tradition nearest to what the Buddha himself taught. There has been some development in Britain, but this has largely become a peculiarly Western style of Buddhism.

The later form, known as Mahayana, is more broadly-based, and has an appeal for a far greater number of people. It does not make such a sharp distinction between lay people and monks, and it has encouraged its followers to get away from the idea that in order to be a good Buddhist one must leave the ordinary world behind and become a monk.

Although Buddhism is a fascinating religious philosophy to study, it is doubtful whether it is a suitable faith to introduce at any depth in the primary school, because of the difficulty and abstract nature of its central beliefs. Some Buddhist rituals and ceremonies could be explored, and there are some marvellous stories found in Buddhist tradition; but the heart of it is not really within the reach of children of primary school age.

Sikhism

Sikhism is a comparatively new religion, when set alongside those described above. It began with the teachings of a man called Nanak in the Punjab area of India, during the late fifteenth and early sixteenth centuries. To those teachings were added other features which were drawn out of the kind of life-style followed by the people in that area at that time, and eventually a third influence was felt, linked with the actual history of the Punjab. Much that is found in Sikhism has more to do with Indian culture than with the doctrines of Sikhs, and there are aspects of the religion in which we can see clear signs of the influence of Hinduism.

Nanak (referred to as Guru Nanak, 'guru' meaning 'teacher') taught that God is a unity, and this idea is symbolised by the appearance of the figure 1 at the opening of the Sikh Holy Book. The aim of the religion is to enter into such a close and intimate relationship with this one God that the worshipper experiences 'salvation'. Man cannot know God in his entirety, but there are certain limited things which can be perceived. For example, God can be seen within creation, if one has the eyes of faith. The inherent danger, however, is that instead of mastering the world, man could become enslaved by it and hopelessly attached to it. So the Sikh tries to tread a delicate path between reverencing God's creation and becoming overwhelmed by it.

Guru Nanak had a strong dislike of anything that looked like ritual or ceremonial. For him, the religious life had nothing to do with such things as pilgrimages, temple rites, or living the life of a recluse. The true place of worship is within the human heart, where man is meant to 'grow into God'.

There were ten gurus altogether, and they have been likened to a succession of candles, each one lit from the flame of its predecessor. Later gurus found it necessary to change direction to some extent, as a result of the circumstances of their time, but they always tried not to lose sight of Guru Nanak's first principles. However, political events and severe persecution made it essential for the Sikh movement to organise itself more rigidly and efficiently. In 1699 the Khalsa was formed, and it became the centre for Sikh religious community life. Boys and girls, on reaching the age of about 14, may become full members of the Khalsa through an initiation ceremony which has been loosely compared to baptism. The Khalsa is a brotherhood or order, in which all religious, moral and political responsibilities come together in a single system. Out of this came the familiar symbols of Sikhism, known as the Five K's: *kesh* (uncut hair), *kangha* (a comb, to hold the long hair in place), *kirpan* (dagger), *kara* (wearing of a steel bangle), and *kachh* (wearing a pair of knee-length trousers). All of these are customarily required. The wearing of a turban is not actually specified as a duty, but it is made necessary by the rule about uncut hair, and has virtually become a religious requirement for practical reasons. At the centre of worship within the Khalsa lies the Sikh Holy Book, known as the Adi Granth. This is kept in the temple (the gurdwara), and when both the people and the Book are met together it is taught that the presence of the Guru is realised.

Today, Sikhs live mainly in the Punjab, but they very much like to travel. Despite their relatively small numbers they are very influential, and are politically active in seeking to have the Punjab marked out as their own land. They tend to enjoy a comparatively high economic standard in comparison with others from the Indian sub-continent, and this may be due to their freedom from those customs which, in other cultures, sometimes inhibit development. However, their readiness to travel and migrate in search of advancement has resulted in the gradual erosion of some of their traditional ways, and many Sikhs in the Western world have given up some or all of the outward symbols of their religion, and have become more integrated into their new environment.

CHAPTER 15

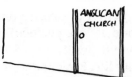

THE MAIN CHRISTIAN DENOMINATIONS

Once again, as with the world's major religions, there are far too many Christian denominations, sects and groups to cover here. We have to be selective, and the policy adopted is therefore to include only those which are generally regarded as the mainstream branches of the contemporary Christian church in Britain.

Basically there are three types of church most evident in this country: the Roman Catholic, the Anglican, and the Free churches. We can look at each of these in turn.

The Roman Catholic church

There are more than 600 million members of the Roman Catholic church throughout the world, but only a very small proportion of them (somewhere around 1 per cent of that figure) live in Britain. The word 'catholic' means 'worldwide', so the church's name actually suggests the idea of a universal church with Rome as the centre. However, when people use the term 'Catholic', they are usually referring to this particular church. Rome is the historical base, because in the early centuries it was the heart of the Roman Empire, and the Christian congregation there was the most influential.

The Roman Catholic church retains the traditions which were characteristic of Western Christianity prior to the Reformation of the sixteenth century. In fact, until the Reformation virtually all churches were Roman Catholic. One of those traditions has been that the Bishop of Rome shall be looked upon as the final authority in matters of spiritual leadership; today he is more familiarly known as the Pope, a word which means 'Father', and it is claimed that he stands in direct succession from St Peter, who is thought to have been the first Bishop of Rome.

The Pope is assisted and advised by the cardinals, who are chosen by him and today have a mainly administrative function. Their number is in theory made up of bishops, priests and deacons, but in practice most are bishops. They have special functions to perform, the most far-reaching being that of meeting in secret on the death of a Pope, in order to choose his successor.

Authority then moves downwards through the various ranks, eventually to the priest of the local parish. It is a principle of Roman Catholicism that this system represents the divine authority, and obedience to it is part of a Catholic's duty.

A feature of this church is its devotion to Mary, the mother of Jesus, and also to particular saints. These personalities are also respected in other branches of the Christian church, but they are usually not venerated to the same extent.

According to Roman Catholic traditional teaching, the priesthood must always be male and unmarried. This is one of the areas of current debate, affecting the question of any possible union between the Roman Catholic and other Christian denominations.

There is one particular teaching in the Roman Catholic church which marks it out from the others, and that concerns what is popularly known as the service of Holy Communion, but in the Roman Catholic tradition is called the Mass. Catholics are taught that after the special bread has been consecrated ('separated out' for a holy purpose), it actually becomes the body of Jesus Christ, even though it still looks like bread. This doctrine is known as transubstantiation, which literally means to cross from being one substance into another. The churches which grew up after the Reformation disagree with this teaching, although in some 'high' Anglican churches the doctrine is still held.

When writing or speaking to a Catholic priest, the conventional form of address is 'Father', followed by either his Christian name or his surname.

The Anglican church

Properly speaking, the word 'Anglican' applies to all churches which accept the authority of the Archbishop of Canterbury, and these include not only the Church of England but also others which are outside this country altogether. There are Anglican churches in Ireland, Wales, Scotland, and even as far away as South Africa and Japan. The Church of England is the only one of the Anglican churches which is still 'established', that is, linked formally with the state. As head of state, the Queen is the nominal head of the Church of England, though in practice she plays very little part in its actual government. Bishops are entitled to sit in the House of Lords, and thus become involved in the government of the country. Leaders of other churches do not have this automatic right. Some regard this arrangement as a constructive partnership between the church and the state, but others see it as a disadvantage, especially when from time to time the church feels it a duty to be critical of political decisions.

It was during the sixteenth century that many people started seriously to question the right of the Pope in Rome to govern churches in other countries, and out of this questioning there came that great ecclesiastical upheaval known as the Reformation. The actual pattern of life within the Church of England was established, not by Henry VIII as many suppose, but by Elizabeth I. She tried to bring together her divided nation by devising a church which would leave room both for those who wished to remain loyal to what was best in the Roman Catholic tradition, and for those who were critical of priestly authority. This is why the spectrum of views within the Church of England today is so broad.

The teachings of the Anglican church are very much like those of the Roman Catholic church, but without the recognition of the authority of the Pope. Every Sunday the Apostles' Creed is repeated during Anglican worship, and this affirms continuity with the early Christian tradition. Another important distinction is that Anglican priests are permitted to marry, and it has recently been decided to admit women into the priesthood – though this is still a somewhat controversial area.

In the Anglican service of Holy Communion, most churches reject the doctrine that the bread becomes the actual body of Christ, so this also marks them out from the Catholic teaching. In addition, Anglicans recognise only two major sacraments (Baptism and Holy Communion), whereas the Roman Catholic church recognises seven.

The Archbishop of Canterbury does not exercise such a strong degree of authority as does the Pope in matters of church government. Nor is the church entirely free to do what it chooses, because of its links with the state. Major changes can be proposed, but these cannot be put into effect without parliamentary approval.

When writing to Anglican clergy, the most usual form of address is 'Reverend John Brown'; it is incorrect to use the title 'Reverend' followed immediately by a surname only ('Reverend Brown'). 'Dear Vicar' or 'Dear Rector' is perfectly proper, but 'Reverend Sir' is very archaic, and 'Dear Reverend' is plain nonsense. Even a simple 'Dear Mr Brown' would not be likely to cause offence.

The Free churches

The Free churches are those which are neither Roman Catholic nor Anglican. They are called 'Free' because of their right to govern themselves as they wish, and not because they believe whatever takes their fancy. Sometimes they are referred to as the Nonconformist churches, but that title is unpopular because it sounds negative rather than positive. Conventionally the main Free churches are:

> The Methodists
> The Baptists
> The United Reformed Church.

The Methodist church

The Methodist church was founded by John Wesley in the eighteenth century. He was actually an Anglican clergyman himself, and did not really want to set up a separate kind of church; he meant Methodism to be a society within the Church of England, but after his death it became an independent group. Today it is calculated that there are over 20 million Methodist church members across the world, and many more adherents. The main authority is the Methodist Conference, made up of 350 ministers and an equal number of laypeople. Beneath it is the Synod, which meets twice each year, and then a further succession of councils, each representing a narrower group of interests. Finally there is an important council, consisting of the members of the local congregation. There is a strong emphasis upon evangelical preaching and upon participation by the church members: Methodism is especially well known for its tradition of hymn-singing. It also has a very strong social conscience.

The Baptist churches

Some readers may wonder why the word 'churches' is used here, rather than 'church' in the singular; the reason is that Baptist churches are all self-governing, and there is no formalised central authority which can tell any of them what to do. All decisions are made by the congregation of the local church, including that of choosing and appointing a minister. There is a co-ordinating organisation called the Baptist Union, but this is not a law-making body. It simply helps the individual congregations to work together and to help one another in such matters as financial support or ministerial training. On the international level there is the Baptist World Alliance, which again facilitates fellowship between the autonomous churches in different countries. Inevitably there are difficulties about calculating membership when churches are distinct from one another, but the Baptist World Alliance has put the number of Baptists, worldwide, at about 30 million.

The distinctive feature of a Baptist church, as its name suggests, is its teaching about baptism. It is committed to the view that the sacrament of baptism is ineffective if the person being baptised is incapable of affirming his or her own faith, and of course this would naturally be true of infants. So infant baptism is never carried out, and in its place is 'believers' baptism', administered when the candidate is able to make a personal commitment, and almost always by the process of total immersion rather than sprinkling.

The United Reformed church

The United Reformed church, known more generally as the URC, is a recent arrival on the British ecclesiastical scene. It was formed in 1972, as a result of a union between the Congregational church and the Presbyterian church of England, both of which trace their origins back to the time of the Reformation. It represents something of a mid-way position between Methodists and Baptists, in terms of its form of government. Each local congregation, like the Baptists, has a degree of independence and is able to make its own decisions about its local affairs. But major decisions have to be referred to the wider councils of the church, somewhat in the manner of Methodism. Since its formation it has been extended by the addition of Christians from other smaller groups.

There are many other denominations which count as being among the Free churches, such as the Society of Friends ('Quakers'), the Salvation Army, and the Pentecostal churches. Details of what they represent can be found by reference to the books recommended in Chapter 18.

Ministers in the Free churches are not priests; they do not officiate at an altar (there are none in the Free church tradition), and they do not consider themselves to be significantly different, in the religious sense, from ordinary church members. They are entitled to be addressed as 'Reverend' in the same way as the clergy of the Anglican church, but it is incorrect to speak of them as 'vicars'. Sometimes the term 'pastor' is used in the smaller denominations. In the case of the Salvation Army the terminology is more military in form, reflecting the original nature of the organisation, and the leaders usually carry a higher rank such as captain or brigadier.

CHAPTER 16

CHRISTIAN SYMBOLS AND THEIR MEANING

Earlier in this book it was suggested that a fruitful approach in teaching RE in the primary school is to explore signs and symbols, not only those used in Christianity, but also in other religious traditions. This is possible, however, only when the teacher has a reasonable grasp of what these symbols are and what they mean. This section provides information about some of the most widely used Christian symbols, and it is hoped that from this starting point teachers will be able to extend the range of their knowledge into other faiths. In some of the illustrations given here, the symbol is actually found in other religions too.

The cross

This is by far the most familiar Christian symbol, and it appears in a great many forms. It represents Christ himself, and it can also stand for the Christian religion. The most common forms of the cross are the Latin and the Greek (see below). The St Andrew cross is shaped like the letter X. Sometimes, especially in old paintings and inscriptions, the cross is designed like the letter T (the Tau cross), and crosses of this shape were commonly used for executions. According to long-established tradition, Jesus was put to death on a cross of the Latin type.

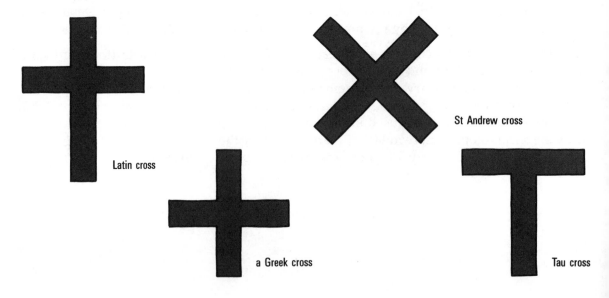

Latin cross

a Greek cross

St Andrew cross

Tau cross

110

The crucifix

Also known as the rood, the crucifix is a representation of Christ actually nailed to the cross. In churches where there is a screen marking the entry to the sanctuary, a crucifix can often be seen on it, and in such cases it is called the rood screen. Crucifixes are more commonly found in Roman Catholic churches than in those of the Reformation tradition; Free churches almost never have one, preferring to display an empty cross signifying the resurrection.

The chi rho symbol

This looks like the letters X and P arranged in the form of a monogram, but it is really made up of the Greek letters *chi* (X) and *rho* (P). They are taken from the beginning of the Greek word *Christos* (Christ).

The fish

The fish is a very ancient symbol, again derived from a combination of Greek letters. The early creed or statement of faith, 'Jesus Christ, God's Son, Saviour', when written in Greek, could be arranged so that the initial letter of each word was extracted and then put with the others to form the word *ichthus*, which is Greek for 'fish'. It was often used as a secret symbol, to denote the presence of a Christian group in an area where such fellowships were not allowed by law to meet.

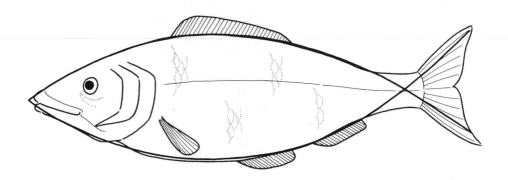

The dove

The dove is a familiar symbol, usually representing peace. It comes from the story of Noah and the Flood (see Genesis 8); but it has also been widely used to represent the Holy Spirit (see Gospel of John 1:32), and it can also signify purity.

The eagle

This symbol has several applications. It is the special symbol of St John (because his ideas seemed to soar so high). It is also commonly found in the design of lecterns (Bible stands) in churches, to represent the concept of God's Word flying to all parts of the earth. Sometimes the eagle symbol is found on baptismal fonts, where it suggests new life and strength. Very occasionally it was used to picture the idea of Christian charity, because according to an ancient legend the eagle would always leave half of its prey for other birds to eat.

The lamb

The lamb is a favourite symbol for Christ who was called 'the Lamb of God' in the Gospel of John, 1:29. Sometimes the symbol represents the whole of sinful humanity, with Christ pictured as the Good Shepherd taking care of his flock. Less often, a ram was a symbol for Christ as the 'chief sheep' of the flock, and as a symbol for his strength.

Trees

Trees are a common symbol in Christianity, but there is no predominant form in which they are used. Sometimes they represent the idea of life, though there are also instances where they symbolise death, usually through association with the 'tree' or cross on which Jesus was crucified.

Fire

Fire can have many meanings. Sometimes it stands for God, and at other times it represents purification, purging or judgement. Quite often it symbolises martyrdom, but it is by no means unusual to find it signifying the religious enthusiasm of saints and prophets. As in the case of the dove, it can be an image of the Holy Spirit: this is what lies behind the curious design of a bishop's headgear (the mitre), which is flame-shaped to suggest the presence of God's spirit upon him as his authority. This is one of the symbols which is found in other religions.

Water

Water is a symbol of cleansing and purifying, but it is also suggestive of drowning (as in the case of a baptismal ceremony, where the meaning is 'death preceding new life'). Sometimes water is a symbol of life itself ('the water of life'), and this is found commonly in many religions.

Candles

Candles are used in several ways, and the meaning of the symbol depends upon the way in which they are employed. The actual flame is associated with the imagery of fire, but it can also suggest the prayers of the faithful rising up to God. Candles are often placed in groups, and the number of candles in the group then becomes significant. Three represent the Holy Trinity. Six placed together on an altar represent constant prayer. In the Roman Catholic tradition, seven candles stand for the seven sacraments. The Paschal candle is placed on a very large candlestick in the north side of the church sanctuary, and lit at special times during the Easter period, then extinguished after the reading of the Gospel on Ascension Day.

Ladders

Ladders sometimes represent prayer (rising up to reach God), but a single ladder can also point to the crucifixion of Jesus in the context of the removal of his body after his death. Occasionally pincers and nails are linked with it to add extra symbolic detail. There is also a connection with the story of Jacob's dream in Genesis 28:3.

In addition to the symbols illustrated here, there is symbolism to be found in the clothes worn by priests and ministers, in the structure of church services (the 'liturgy'), in the actions of the worshippers, and even in the design of the whole building. Teachers are strongly advised to refer to specialist sources in order to take full advantage of this rich vein of teaching material.

Baptist Missionary Society, 93 Gloucester Place, London W1H 4AA
BBC Publications, 35 Marylebone High Street, London W1M 4AA
Board of Deputies of British Jews, Woburn House, Upper Woburn Place, London WC1H 0EP
British Council of Churches, 2 Eaton Gate, London SW1
British and Foreign Bible Society, 146 Queen Victoria Street, London EC4V 4BX
British Mahabodhi Society, London Buddhist Vihara, 5 Heathfield Gardens, London W4 4JV
British Red Cross, 9 Grosvenor Crescent, London SW1
Buddhist Centre, 51 Roman Road, London E2
Buddhist Society, 58 Eccleston Square, London SW1

Catholic Education Council, 41 Cromwell Road, London SW7
Catholic Fund for Overseas Development (CAFOD), 2 Romero Close, London SW9 9TY
Central Office of Information, Hercules Road, London SE1 7DU
Centre for World Development Education, Inner Circle, Regents Park, London NW1
Cheshire (Leonard) Foundation, 26 Maunsel Street, London W1
Christian Action, 308 Kennington Lane, London SE11
Christian Aid, 240 Ferndale Road, London SW9
Christian Education Movement, Lancaster House, Borough Road, Isleworth, Middlesex (Video
    Dept: 5 Dean Street, London W1V 5RN)
Church Missionary Society, 157 Waterloo Road, London SE1 8UU
Commission for Racial Equality, Elliott House, 10–12 Allington Street, London SW1 5EH
Commonwealth Institute, Kensington High Street, London W8 6NQ
Concord Films Council Ltd, 210 Felixstowe Road, Ipswich, Suffolk

Educational Foundation for Visual Aids, Unit 5, The Sidings, Hainault Road, London E11

Help the Aged, Education Department, 8/10 Denman Street, London W1A 2AP
Hindu Centre, 39 Grafton Terrace, London NW5

India Book Centre, 52 Tytherton Road, London N19
Indian Government Tourist Office, 7 Cork Street, London W1
Institute of Race Relations, 2 Leeke Street, London WC1
Islamic Centre, 10 Berwick Street, London W1
Islamic Culture and Education Centre, 75 Falcon Road, London SW11
Islamic Cultural Centre and London Mosque, Regent's Lodge, 146 Park Road, London NW8
Islamic Publications, London Mosque, 16 Gressenhall Road, London SW18
Israel Art and Craft, 146a Golders Green Road, London NW11

Jewish Education Bureau, 8 Westcombe Avenue, Leeds LS8 2BS
Jewish National Fund, Harold Poster House, Kingsbury Circle, London NW9
Jewish Memorial Council and Jewish Museum, Books Dept, Woburn House, Upper Woburn Place, London WC1

Mission to Seamen, St Michael Paternoster Royal, College Hill, London EC4
Muslim Educational Trust, 130 Stroud Green Road, London N4

National Children's Home, 85 Highbury Park, London N5
National Christian Education Council, Robert Denholm House, Nutfield, Redhill, Surrey RH1 4HW
NSPCC, 67 Saffron Hill, London EC1
National Union of Teachers, Publications Dept, Hamilton House, Mabledon Place, London WC1H 9BD

Oxfam, 274 Banbury Road, Oxford, OX2 7DZ

Pictorial Charts Educational Trust, 27 Kirchen Road, West Ealing, London W13 0UD

Royal National Institute for the Blind, 224 Great Portland Street, London W1N 6AA
Royal National Institute for the Deaf, 105 Gower Street, London WC1
RSPCA, Manor House, Causeway, Horsham, Sussex RH12 1HG

Samaritans, Griffin House, High Street, Bracknell, Berks.
Save the Children Fund, Mary Datchelor House, 17 Grove Lane, London SE5
Shaftesbury Society, 2a Amity Grove, London SW20
Shelter, 88 Old Street, London EC1
Sikh Cultural Society, 88 Mollison Way, Edgware, Middlesex

The Slide Centre, 17 Broderick Road, London SW17
TEAR Fund, 90 Church Road, Teddington, Middlesex

War on Want, 37 Great Guildford Street, London SE1

Names and addresses of the main Christian churches/denominations in Britain, listed in alphabetical order:

The following addresses refer to the *central offices, publishing houses, and/or education departments* of the churches identified, from which general information can be obtained. Correspondence with individual congregations should be sent directly to the local priest, minister or leader.

Assemblies of God in Great Britain and Ireland, 106–114 Talbot Street, Nottingham NG1 5GH

Baptist Church Information, 139 Grosvenor Avenue, London N5
Baptist Union of Great Britain and Ireland, 4 Southampton Row, London WC1B 4AB

Catholic Truth Society, 38/40 Eccleston Square, London SW1
Church Army, Winchester House, Independents Road, London SE3
Church of England, Church House, Dean's Yard, London SW1P 3NZ
Church of Ireland, Church of Ireland House, Church Avenue, Rathmines, Dublin 6
Church of Scotland, 121 George Street, Edinburgh 2
Church in Wales, 39 Cathedral Road, Cardiff CF1 9XF
Congregational Federation, 12 Canal Street, Nottingham NG1 7EH
Congregational Union of Scotland, 1 University Avenue, Glasgow G12 8NN

Elim Pentecostal Churches, 117 St Georges Road, Cheltenham, Gloucestershire
Episcopal Church in Scotland, 21 Grosvenor Crescent, Edinburgh EH12 5EE

Methodist Church, 1 Central Buildings, Matthew Parker Street, Westminster, London SW1
Methodist Church, Division of Education, 2 Chester House, Pages Lane, London N10

Orthodox Churches, The Fellowship of St Alban and St Sergius, 52 Ladbroke Grove, London
    W11 2PB

Plymouth Brethren, 1 Widcombe Crescent, Bath, Avon
Presbyterian Church in Ireland, Church House, Fisherwick Place, Belfast, N. Ireland BT1 6DW
Presbyterian Church of Wales, 9 Camden Road, Brecon, LD3 7BU

Quakers (Society of Friends), Friends House, Euston Road, London NW1 2BJ

Salvation Army, 101 Queen Victoria Street, London EC4 4EP

United Reformed Church, 86 Tavistock Place, London WC1H 9RT
Unitarian Headquarters, 1 Essex Street, London WC2

CHAPTER
18

RESOURCES FOR RELIGIOUS EDUCATION

When the word 'resources' is mentioned, the natural tendency is to think in terms of books and audio-visual aids, which can be kept in school and brought out as the occasion demands. In reality, however, the term covers much more than that. Books do matter, and so do pictures, videos, photographic slides and artefacts; but beyond these conventional items there are many other things which can be regarded as resources yet are often overlooked. For example, *people* are resources. In almost every locality there are folk who have experience or expertise in matters of religion, and who would readily respond to an invitation to contribute to the children's learning by visiting the school. Ministers and clergy are familiar examples, but there may be people in the area who, for instance, have retired after working abroad, or who have some special kind of experience which they would be willing to share with the children. The identity of such people can only be discovered by 'asking around' in such places as local churches, libraries, the social services, or in other schools. Teachers can build up lists of suitable visitors as a resource reference for use in programme planning.

Also, *buildings* are resources. In Chapter 12 we discussed the practicalities of visiting a place of worship, but other kinds of buildings such as memorial halls and stately homes frequently have much to offer. Some actually have chapels contained within them. Monuments, too, can be drawn to the children's attention; large numbers of these stand in public places around the landscape and yet are largely unrecognised until their purpose is explained.

Other curriculum areas can also provide resources which are useful in RE work. Because a book is placed in the library under the label 'history' or 'geography', it does not follow that it has no value outside these fields. As we have stressed earlier, what makes something 'religious' is not so much what it is as how it is used. The same principle holds good when teachers are previewing slides or videos or television programmes.

Yet, having acknowledged that resources can be of many kinds, it remains true that teachers generally appreciate guidance concerning the most conventional kind – books. So what follows is a list of suggested titles, separated out under the headings 'Resources for the teacher' and 'Resources for the children'. The teachers' material might eventually be put together to form a staffroom collection, which the RE coordinator could oversee and supplement from time to time. Much of what is recommended for the children could be placed in the school library for classes to borrow, rather than hidden away in stock cupboards. The items listed are no more than a very small selection from a very large range currently available; to produce an exhaustive list would be both unwieldy and unrealistic. Visual aids such as slide packs, videos and wallcharts are not included, because it is important that teachers should actually see these rather than merely know of their existence. Most RE resources centres have facilities for viewing items of this nature. The names and addresses of some publishers of visual materials can be found in Chapter 17, and they will usually respond to requests for catalogues.

Resources for the teacher

Basic reference books and handbooks

The Local Authority's Agreed Syllabus for RE.

The Bible in English, preferably in several different versions.

A concordance to the Bible. This is a kind of dictionary to facilitate finding particular words, themes or passages.

An atlas of the Bible. A contemporary world atlas will not be suitable, because many ancient religious sites have now disappeared or have changed their names. *Religious Education Atlas* (Jan Thompson: Edward Arnold, 1986) is useful.

A Bible encyclopaedia is a good tool for points of detail. *The Oxford Companion to the Bible* (OUP, 1993) is excellent, if somewhat specialised, and the *Lion Handbook to the Bible* (first published 1973) is also useful. For looking up unfamiliar terms, see *Religious Education Glossary of Terms: Buddhism, Christianity, Hinduism, Islam, Judaism, Sikhism* (School Curriculum and Assessment Authority, July 1994).

Scriptures of major non-Christian religious, such as the Islamic Qur'an, are useful when teaching about other faiths. These can usually be obtained in inexpensive paperback form.

A calendar of religious festivals is vital if the teacher wishes to make reference to the holy days of particular religions. As many of these occur at different times each year, the calendar needs to be updated annually. The Commission for Racial Equality and the National Union of Teachers both publish these.

General RE books

COLE and EVANS-LOWNDES, *Religious Education and the Primary Curriculum: Teaching Strategies and Practical Activities* (Chansitor Publications, 1995)
HUGHES, Elizabeth, *Religious Education in the Primary School: Managing Diversity* (Cassell, 1994)
JACKSON, R. and STARKINGS, D., *Junior Religious Education Handbook* (Stanley Thornes, 1990)
KEENE, M., *New Steps in Religious Education series* (Stanley Thornes, 1991)
PUMFREY, P. and VERMA, G., *Foundation Subjects and Religious Education in the Primary School* (Falmer Press, 1993)
READ, G. *et al.*, *How Do I Teach RE?* (Stanley Thornes, 1987)
SUTCLIFFE, J. (ed.), *Dictionary of Religious Education* (SCM, 1984)

Basic information about world religions

We have provided a thumbnail sketch of some of the world's major religions (see Chapter 14), but for classroom presentation teachers will need to have access to more information than this. Useful material about the various Christian denominations can be obtained by writing directly to the relevant offices (see list of addresses, pages 118–19). For material on other religions, in addition to the sources listed from page 117 above, the following books will be helpful. Although intended for use in secondary schools, they will serve as excellent guides for the non-specialist teacher.

'Living Religions' series (Ward Lock Educational, 1973–)
> *Sikhism*
> *Hinduism*
> *Judaism*
> *Islam*
> *The Orthodox Church*
> *Roman Catholicism*
> *Protestant Christian Churches*
> *The Rastafarians*

'Christian Denominations' series (Religious and Moral Education Press, 1977–)
> *The Church of England*
> *The Methodist Church*
> *The Church of Scotland*
> *The Brethren*
> *The Orthodox Church*
> *The Society of Friends*
> *The Salvation Army*
> *The Roman Catholic Church*
> *The Pentecostal Churches*
> *The United Reformed Church*
> *The Baptists*

For teachers who wish to gain a more detailed knowledge of world religions, there are several good one-volume guides currently on the market. *The World's Religions* (Lion Handbook, 1994) is helpful, as also is the *Handbook of Living Religions* (John Hinnells: Penguin Paperback, 1991). *World's Religions: Understanding the Living Faiths* (Peter B. Clarke: Readers' Digest books, 1994) is attractively presented. A good permanent reference book for the staffroom library would be the *Larousse Dictionary of Beliefs and Religions* (1992). Also useful is the *Longman Guide to Living Religions* (Ian Harris: 1994).

Books for use with children

'Living Festivals' series (Religious and Moral Education Press, 1983 ongoing)
> *Shabbat*
> *Passover*
> *Saraswati Puja*

Holi
May Day
Harvest and Thanksgiving
Ascensiontide and Pentecost
Succot and Simchat Torah
Baisakhi
Chinese New Year
Hallowe'en, All Souls and All Saints
Advent and Christmas
Shrove Tuesday, Ash Wednesday and Mardi Gras
Holy Week
Easter
Durga Puja
Ramadan and Id-ul-Fitr
Festivals of the Buddha
Hindu Festivals (Teacher's book)
Jewish Festivals (Teacher's book)
Muslim Festivals (Teacher's book)

'Celebrate' series (Heinemann Library, 1995)
    Christian Festivals
    Buddhist Festivals
    Hindu Festivals
    Sikh Festivals

'Discovering Religions' series (Heinemann Library, 1995)
    Sikhism
    Hinduism
    Christianity
    Buddhism
    Islam
    Judaism

'Young Books' series (Simon and Schuster, 1992)
    The Muslim World
    The Hindu World
    The Christian World
    The Jewish World
    The Buddhist World
    The Sikh World
    The New Religions World

    Paperback set – 1 of each of above 7 titles also available

'Religions of the World' series (Wayland, 1986)
Buddhism
Christianity
Hinduism
Islam
Judaism
Sikhism

(see also the same publishers' 'Festivals' series)

'Understanding Religions' series (Wayland, 1992)
Birth Customs
Death Customs
Food and Fasting
Initiation Customs
Marriage Customs
Pilgrimages and Journeys

'Religious Stories' series (Wayland, 1986)
Buddhist Stories
Chinese Stories
Creation Stories
Guru Nanak and the Sikh Gurus
Hindu Stories
Old Testament Stories
The Life of Jesus
The Life of the Buddha
The Life of Muhammad
The Lives of the Saints

'Stories from World Religions' series (Heinemann, 1995)
Birth of the Buddha
Birth of Jesus
Story of Easter
Story at Id
Story of Prahlad
Stories Jesus Told
People Jesus Met
Jews Leave Egypt
Guru Nanak
Moses on the Mountain
Buddha and the Bodhi Tree

(above also available as a Series Pack)

'Westhill Project' series (Stanley Thornes, 1990)
    Life Themes in the Early Years (3 packs)

Also useful:

KIRBY and BLACKMORE *Celebrating the Festivals*, Church Pastoral Aid Society (1990)
MEREDITH, S. *World Religions*, The Usborne Guide (1995)

RE Resources Centres

Teachers are strongly advised to check whether there is an RE Resources Centre within reach of their school. This could be either a Local Education Authority Centre or a Centre funded by local churches and/or religious communities. Such centres are usually well-stocked with up-to-date materials for viewing or borrowing, or even for purchase, and will generally provide specialist professional advice. It may be necessary for the school, or the individual teacher, to pay an affiliation fee or subscription to some of these centres, but it is usually only a nominal amount. In addition, visits to ethnic arts/crafts shops can be very profitable, as also can a careful exploration of conventional stationery shops for such items as greetings cards for various religious festivals and celebrations, e.g., Bar Mitzvah cards, etc. In areas where there is a significant ethnic or religious minority population these shops can be extremely useful, as also can food stores and supermarkets which sell food items associated with the dietary customs of particular religious traditions. Local Christian ministers and clergy will often make items available for loan, such as vestments or artefacts used in services of worship, though sometimes only under strict supervision if the items are especially valuable.

E

SCHOOL WORSHIP

In this final section there is a general discussion of the Act of Collective Worship, which outlines the current legal position. It also includes:

▶ a consideration of the nature of worship

▶ the essential ingredients in an act of worship

▶ practical considerations in planning acts of worship

▶ pointers towards resources for acts of worship.

CHAPTER 19

THE ACT OF COLLECTIVE WORSHIP

The Act of Collective Worship in state schools is quite distinct from the Religious Education carried out in the normal curriculum, both in the legal sense and in terms of its nature and purpose. Although there are similarities deriving from the obvious fact that the two activities are concerned with religious life and belief, it is important that the distinction between them is kept constantly in mind, because they are not the same thing. As we have already noted, Religious Education is concerned with the development of children's insights into the nature of religion, the encouragement of openness and sensitivity towards people's spiritual beliefs and customs, and the development of those skills which are necessary for the appreciation of religious ideas (see Chapter 3). Worship, on the other hand, has to do with the personal acknowledgement of God, and the act of self-giving or commitment to him. Of course it is true that there is an element of education in worship itself, since we learn something from everything we do: but education does not necessarily involve worship. One can learn about religious beliefs and practices without being personally committed to them. It is here that the areas of controversy concerning school worship are most evident.

Attendance at the act of worship

The current legal position is that, in all state-maintained schools, there must be an Act of Collective Worship held on every school day, on school premises. All pupils are required to attend, unless their parents have formally asked that they be withdrawn. If the parents do not make this request, then it is technically illegal for pupils to be held back from the act of worship in order to be given extra reading practice, or to finish off some outstanding piece of work, although this is very commonly done. Where parents do make the request for withdrawal, it must be granted without question, and they do not have to explain or justify their request.

It is also open to teachers to exercise a similar right of withdrawal. They are free to opt out of attendance at the act of worship, and cannot be compelled to be present. However, this freedom applies *only* to those parts of the Assembly which are genuinely religious, such as the singing of hymns and participating in prayers. It does *not* apply to those parts which are purely secular, such as the giving out of school notices; Head Teachers can require all their staff to be present for anything which is not 'worship' in the proper sense.

Head Teachers themselves are also free to refuse to participate in acts of worship, but because they are responsible for the day-to-day running of the school they are still contractually bound to ensure that worship takes place, and, if they will not lead it themselves, they must find someone else to take their place. If they cannot find a qualified teacher to lead the worship, they are permitted to find someone else, provided that the person is competent, and is aware of what the law requires.

Practical arrangements are now more flexible

Under the provisions of the Education Reform Act of 1988 it is now permissible for the Act of Collective Worship to be organised more flexibly than was the case under the previous Education Act of 1944. Pupils may be divided into smaller groups, such as upper and lower school, individual classes, or any other kind of grouping which is used for normal teaching activities. But it is *not* permitted for the pupils to be separated into *religious* groups. Furthermore, whereas under the old system the act of worship was fixed at the beginning of every school day, it is now possible to hold it at any suitable time, although it must take place every day. This flexibility goes a long way towards enabling teachers to focus more clearly upon the specific needs and abilities of the children involved: one of the most difficult problems in earlier times for those who led acts of worship was the need to devise ways of catering for a very wide range of ages and ability levels – quite apart from the logistical awkwardness of coping with a 'congregation' numbering as many as five hundred or more at a time.

If a particular school is populated by children from non-Christian backgrounds, special arrangements can be made for organising acts of worship which are more appropriate to their culture and circumstances. The correct approach is for the Head Teacher to make an alternative proposal to the local Standing Advisory Council on Religious Education (SACRE), who will then either approve or disapprove of that particular proposal. The Council, however, will not engage in discussion or offer advice on the alternative proposal. It is up to the Head Teacher to work out the kind of Act of Collective Worship which would be most relevant in that particular situation.

Acts of worship must be broadly Christian

The law states that, in schools other than those which are accepted as being special cases, the majority of Acts of Collective Worship must be 'wholly or mainly of a broadly Christian character'. This means that the emphasis must be on the broad traditions of Christian belief and must not be narrowly sectarian in nature. It is still illegal for any state-maintained school to organise acts of worship which are distinctive of any particular denomination. However, not every act of worship must be of this Christian nature. Guidelines have been issued indicating that, taking each school term as a whole, the *majority* must be broadly Christian.

What *is* an act of worship?

Although the present law requires that there shall be an Act of Collective Worship held every day in state-maintained schools, it does not specify what an act of worship actually is – and this is where many problems are encountered. Teachers are commonly heard to ask 'What can we do in the Assembly in order to make it genuinely religious?' This is simply another way of asking what it is that should go into an act of worship in order to distinguish it from an RE lesson which has an educational intention. Because of this uncertainty about what it is that constitutes an act of worship, many Assemblies become no more than presentations or performances – often well-planned and executed, but failing to conform to the proper definition of worship.

Worship, in its proper sense, is the act of recognising 'worth' ('*worthship*'). It signifies the business of celebrating and honouring that which is recognised as being 'the highest of all', i.e. that which is of ultimate worth or value. In the Christian tradition, this simply means acknowledging the supremacy of God over everything else and submitting oneself to him.

Informal and formal worship

It has always been recognised that there are two ways of thinking about worship. First, there is the *informal* way, in which life itself is looked upon as a continuous process of 'living for God'. When worship is seen in this way, everything that we do is regarded as being given to God, and no distinction is made between everyday activities and religious devotion. Then there is the *formal* way of regarding worship, in which specific acts or rituals are performed, at certain times and in particular ways. These generally take the form of corporate ceremonies, in which a number of people come together as a congregation to express their religious devotion. The Act of Collective Worship in schools really falls into the second of these two categories, because it is an organised and distinct activity or celebration, in which the whole school participates, and it is carried out in a way which distinguishes it from other 'normal' activities. Nevertheless, it does not preclude the possibility of also encouraging a 'worshipful' approach to the whole of the day's work, and indeed there are many people who believe that this is one of its most important purposes – i.e. to create a spiritual context for the forthcoming day's activities.

The ingredients of worship

Where worship is treated as a specific ceremony or act, it normally contains certain very clear and necessary ingredients. Among these are:

- ▶ belief in God as the 'object' of worship
- ▶ affirmations of faith and trust in God
- ▶ 'conversation' with God through speaking and listening
- ▶ self-offering or 'promising' oneself to God.

If any of these elements is missing, then genuine worship is not taking place at all. We can consider each of them in turn.

Belief in God as the object of worship

If the act of worship is not consciously, explicitly and deliberately directed towards God, then it fails in its purpose and it becomes something quite different. If it is not openly addressed to God, then at least in the Christian sense it is not worship at all. Here we encounter one of the most controversial issues in the entire debate about school worship: are young children capable of genuine belief, that is to say, belief which is really their own, and which is not merely a repetition of dogmas imposed on them by other authority figures? The answers to this are far from settled, and there is still room for continuing discussion. They involve questions of the meaning of religious maturity, and the nature of belief itself, which we cannot discuss here.

Another closely related problem lies in the fact that a state-maintained school is not in itself a religious community, and there will almost certainly be pupils within it who have no clearly formulated religious convictions at all. To require them to engage in an act of worship is impossible, since, because they do not have any awareness of God or belief in him they cannot meaningfully address him in the context of genuine worship. The best that they can be expected to do is to involve themselves empathetically with others for whom genuine worship is possible. By doing this, they are gaining insights into what an act of worship entails, and they may well be learning *how* to worship, but they are not *worshipping* in the proper sense. This is a particularly difficult area of debate at the present time, and there is no clear consensus of opinion emerging.

However, this does imply that whoever is leading the act of worship ought to take into account the difficulty which many of the children may be finding in focusing upon 'God', and in practical terms this may mean that some brief explanatory introduction is needed from time to time. This could take the form of a simple statement such as, 'Those of you who find it hard to picture what God is like, or find it hard to talk to him, might wish to think about some of the things that are most important to you, and be glad about them'. There is no value whatsoever in disciplining young children for their inability to sustain the traditional and conventional postures of worship – 'hands together and eyes closed'. Indeed, to insist too strongly upon conformity to outward observances, even though there is no inner conviction, is at worst to encourage hypocrisy, or at best to perpetuate the impression that worship is nothing more than empty ritual.

Affirmations of faith and trust in God

These form part of any true act of worship. In effect, they consist of statements of the worshipper's acknowledgement of God's power, and the most usual form of their expression is through the singing of appropriate hymns. Such old favourites as *All Things Bright and Beautiful* or *Praise to the Lord, the Almighty, the King of Creation* obviously embody these sentiments, but these particular hymns are becoming increasingly dated, and every effort should be made to identify more modern hymns which contain the same essential ideas.

But hymns are not the only medium through which the children can be brought closer to an acknowledgement of God's creative and sustaining power. This can also be silently affirmed by the *environment* in which the act of worship is taking place. To surround the children with pictures or objects of beauty, and to create an atmosphere of reverence through the use of suitable music, is also crucially important. Buildings such as churches, mosques or synagogues, which have been set apart specifically for the purpose of worship, are always dignified and beautified in appropriate ways, yet many school Assemblies take place in a hall or room where no attempt has been made to create a sense that this is a special occasion, or that something very special is being done. Obviously this cannot be taken very far, because of the functional nature of the premises, but even a few minor touches can make a great deal of difference. If it is hard to encourage young children to appreciate the things that are good and beautiful and worthwhile, no useful purpose is served by making it even harder through neglecting to have any of these things in evidence!

In the same vein, the physical conditions in which the children are expected to engage in worship will have an effect upon their ability to respond to invitations to 'meet with God'. If they are seated uncomfortably on the floor, pressed tightly against each other, unable to see what is going on at the front, or distracted by other activities taking place within their line of vision, then it will not be surprising to find that the atmosphere of worship is either totally absent or at best very difficult to sustain. Now that the Education Reform Act has given schools the freedom to organise the Act of Collective Worship in any way which is deemed appropriate, there is no longer any good reason why more thought cannot be given to creating a worshipful and stimulating setting. Schools which are fortunate enough to have sufficiently large premises could perhaps look at the possibility of setting one large room aside specifically as a worship area, into which individual classes or groups can come.

Conversation with God

Every act of worship is essentially a kind of dialogue. The worshipper speaks to God, and listens to what God has to say to him or her. At first this seems an impossible encounter for a humble state-maintained school to arrange, but much depends upon how the leader perceives it. There are two aspects to this: the first has to do with devising ways in which the children can try to 'talk to God', and the second has to do with appreciating how, in people's religious experience, God commonly 'talks to us'.

When people are engaged in worship, they usually do such things as saying prayers or singing hymns. These are the most familiar ways of 'talking to God'. Prayers are simply ordinary words, carefully chosen because they are addressed to God, and used to communicate the things that matter most to the God who matters most. They can be prayers in which the worshipper admits his or her personal weaknesses and failings (prayers of *Confession*). The important thing about these is that they must be honest. Young children do not always have a very acute sense of personal wrong-doing, especially when they are still trying to formulate their own autonomous standards of morality: but they can be helped to acknowledge such faults as selfishness, laziness, lack of thought for others, or failing to respect their environment. Then there are prayers in which acknowledgement is made of the things that have been done for us – prayers of gratitude (*Thanksgiving*). By this means, the children can be brought to an awareness of what it means to be loved and cared for, and encouraged to do the same for other people. Prayers of *Intercession* are really prayers in which the children think about other people and their needs. These do not have to be large-scale concerns, like asking God to help to bring international peace: indeed, young children generally find it very difficult to conceptualise such major or distant issues. It is sufficient for them to focus upon the needs of the people they know – family members, friends, or teachers, and to attempt to empathise with them. Alongside prayers of intercession are those which are usually called *Petition* – asking God for specific things. Care must be taken here, because it is easy to lapse into silliness, such as asking God to provide good weather for the school Sports Day, or asking for success in forthcoming examinations. But part of the discipline of prayer is that of learning the difference between what we can properly ask from God and what God expects responsible people to do for themselves.

Many schools have found it very rewarding to encourage pupils to compose their own prayers, and then to put these together for use in a corporate or collective setting. There is no such thing as a special prayer-language: all that matters is that the sentiments shall be sincere.

A study of any collection of hymns will show that prayers can frequently be embodied in the form of hymns, and when children are learning new hymns it is important that they focus as clearly upon the words as they do upon the tunes, so that they can be helped to sing with understanding as well as with enthusiasm.

But talking to God is only one side of the dialogue. Listening is the other side, and this immediately raises the question of how a worship-leader can arrange for God to speak to the children. It seems arrogant even to claim that it can be done. But it is the Christian experience that God does not normally 'speak' to people through such dramatic happenings as heavenly voices or angelic visitations: he speaks through very ordinary and mundane things. God's word is embodied in everything that is true and loving. It is heard in the pleadings of the poor and oppressed people of the world, and in the voices of those who are working to care for them. It is heard in everything that is beautiful or worthwhile. It is heard in stories of the lives or deeds of people who serve others, or who sacrifice themselves for the sake of their fellows. So an act of worship will contain all these elements, because a Christian will affirm that it is through them that God speaks to us. There will sometimes be carefully selected readings from the Bible, chosen with an awareness of the children's ability to understand. There will be stories, factual or fictional, which communicate truth or which exemplify love in operation. There is an enormously rich well of material to be tapped in the field of biography, fable, and general history. Again, God's word can come through drama, or music, or poetry, or through the recounted experiences of a visitor to the school who has something to share with the children. At the end of this chapter the reader will find a discussion of some of the resources which can be tapped in order to provide material for school worship – resources which in the majority of cases the school will already possess.

Making promises to God

Finally, in every act of worship there is a point at which the worshipper makes some kind of personal commitment. This is usually in the form of a renewal of Christian discipleship, but it need not be as formalised as that. In essence it is an undertaking to do better – to try harder or to aim higher. This is the part within an act of worship where the individual renews his or her first promises:

O Jesus, I have promised
to serve thee to the end;
be thou for ever near me,
my Master and my friend.

Here we touch upon the whole point and purpose of worship, which is to respond to God by doing our best. In the context of the Primary school this need not be over-formalised in the conventional religious sense. It can be no more than an element of encouragement to maintain or even surpass the standards set within the life of the school – to work together more effectively, to develop a sense of community, to pursue the highest aims and objectives, and to use individual gifts and talents for the common good. Even those children who find it hard to accept traditional religious beliefs can share in this aspect of worship, because for them it will simply be a promise to try harder and to do better.

Pitfalls to avoid when planning school worship

Like any other school activity, there are certain hazards to be avoided when planning the Act of Collective Worship. These can be listed very briefly:

1   Acts of worship are at their best when they are kept as simple as possible. The more complicated the arrangements, the more there is that can go wrong, and the greater the difficulty of maintaining a reverential atmosphere. To turn the Assembly into an opportunity to 'put on a little play' is ill-advised, especially when it involves the use of costumes, scenery, and the learning of words from a script. This is acceptable for purposes of dramatic presentations, but it has to be kept in mind that an act of worship is *not* the same thing as a concert.

2   Careful thought should be given before adopting the widely followed custom of having a weekly or monthly 'Parents' Assembly', to which members of the children's families are invited. This can, of course, contribute to good relationships between the school and the parents, but it can also result in the act of worship turning into a 'show', with the parents as the audience. In the world of religion, people do not normally go to watch an act of worship taking place; they go to participate in it. It is *not* a spectator activity, and when the children know that their parents are watching them, they lose sight of the fact that they are supposed to be addressing their activities towards God.

3   Where a school operates a system of class Assemblies, in which each class is responsible for planning and producing acts of worship for presentation to the whole school, there is an inherent danger that these can become quite blatantly competitive, with one class trying to outdo another in the quality of the activity. This is especially likely when the act of worship is made to consist very largely of a demonstration of the work which has been going on in that particular class, on the basis of 'Look what we've been doing!' Although there is a good case to be made for bringing the work of the class into the open, for others to see and share, and to present it in a way which suggests that it has been done to the glory of God, the inherent risks should also be taken into account and weighed in the balance.

4   There is no reason whatsoever for assuming that the quality of an act of worship is to be measured in terms of its duration. An Assembly which lasts for an hour is not necessarily better than one which lasts for only ten minutes. Indeed, there is much to be said for keeping it as short as possible, because one of the most common complaints levelled against a compulsory act of worship is that it eats into precious teaching time. Furthermore, it is very difficult to sustain genuine worship for a long period, especially where young children are involved.

5   When the Act of Collective Worship was required to be held at the start of each school day, there was an inevitable tendency for it to be used as a time when the Head Teacher would 'hold the fort', and the class teachers would prepare their rooms for the forthcoming day's activities. This was also sometimes justified on the ground that it provided the Head Teacher with an opportunity to meet the children, when otherwise he or she would be desk-bound. But it has to be remembered that the act of worship was never intended to be used as a holding device: its purpose is to engage the children (and the staff) in a religious activity.

6   The fact that Head Teachers are free to invite visitors from outside the school to lead the acts of worship is, of course, a great benefit. But it, too, has its dangers. There is no shortage of people from religious groups and sects who are anxious to get a foothold in the school and seek to win the children to their particular cause. Sometimes, in the interest of fair play, a Head Teacher will allow such people to come in, and once they arrive it is very difficult to control what they do. It must constantly be kept in mind that the content of the Act of Collective Worship must *not* be in any way sectarian. Again, it often happens that a local minister or clergyman will come in to lead the act of worship, but will have no idea of how to talk to young children in their own language. He (or she) will use abstract or technical terminology, and will be 'over the heads' of most of the children for most of the time. It is always advisable to do some careful checking before inviting anyone into the school for the purpose of leading the Assembly, and to ensure that those who do come are fully aware of the conditions under which they will be working.

7   Because the act of worship is a school-based activity, every effort needs to be made to ensure that what is done is plainly relevant to the life of the school. Unless this is kept in mind, the act of worship will come to be thought of as a kind of irrelevant appendage, and the children will conclude that this is true of all acts of worship in all places. Just as the regular services of worship in churches are closely linked with the total activities of the members of the congregations, so also the Act of Collective Worship in school must be connected with everything else that goes on there.

Resources for school worship

If school worship is to be effective and meaningful it must be properly resourced. Among the most important resources will be the human variety – *people*, from inside and outside the school, who are able to lead worship from a position of personal commitment and professional competence. These might be teachers, clergy or lay people from local congregations, former pupils, or indeed anyone who has a proper sense of what worship is all about, and who can encourage the children to take an active part in it. It is a useful practice to build up a list of the names and addresses of such people as these, so that they can be called upon to help whenever it is appropriate.

Resources will also include visual and aural aids to worship – music, pictures, furnishings and artefacts which can either beautify the environment in which the act of worship takes place, or serve as focal points for prayerful thought and consideration. Even such a simple thing as a loaf of bread can stimulate the children to think about where it comes from, the skills involved in producing it, the plight of people who do not have enough to eat, or the symbolism involved when talking about Jesus as the Bread of Life.

As far as more conventional resources are concerned, the school should be well-equipped with a range of hymnbooks, both traditional and contemporary, supplemented by any worthwhile contributions from the pupils themselves which can be used on more than one occasion. There should be copies of the Bible readily available, in any version, but especially those which are most easily understood by the children. A *Dictionary of Biography* is invaluable (though sometimes quite costly), because from this kind of publication the worship-leader can draw examples of people whose lives or exploits can be used to illustrate how worship can be translated into action. Books from the school's own collection of history resources can often contain material which will serve the purposes of the Assembly very well indeed. Similarly, books on Science will furnish examples of people who used their gifts and skills for the good of humanity, and possibly open up ideas about how the things that we discover can be used either for constructive or destructive purposes. Art materials will feed an Assembly where the focus is on beauty, or the use of our senses. The point here, of course, is that because religion has to do with the whole spectrum of life, the resources for religious worship are derived from virtually anywhere and everywhere. If a school has resources for teaching, it already has resources for worship, because the two purposes are served from the same basic materials.

Collections of Assembly stories are plentiful and easy to obtain: they pour from the religious presses faster than any bibliography can ever be produced. But care should be taken to avoid those which treat religion as nothing more than morality, or which create the impression that everything in the world is beautiful: at some point the children need to come to terms with the fact that there are such things as cruelty and suffering in the world, and that these, too, have a proper place within an act of worship. Sometimes very familiar stories can be looked at in new ways – as, for example, the story of Pinocchio, which is really a Christian parable which makes the point that we are only truly human when we can live with integrity. Items from daily or local newspapers can be used, especially to give the act of worship a topical significance, and obviously there is a wealth of possibility deriving from the television programmes which children generally watch. If we note the way in which the world's great religious leaders have taught, we quickly see that they drew their inspiration, not mainly from holy books or sacred places, but from ordinary, everyday life. The secret lies in seeing what is there, and then translating it into terms of worship.

Index of key words